W9-ACA-771

From Papyrus to Hypertext

TOPICS IN THE DIGITAL HUMANITIES

Humanities computing is redefining basic principles about
research and publication. An influx of new, vibrant, and
diverse communities of practitioners recognizes that computer
applications are subject to continual innovation and reappraisal.
This series publishes books that demonstrate the new questions,
methods, and results arising in the digital humanities.

Series Editors
Susan Schreibman
Raymond C. Siemens

From Papyrus to Hypertext

Toward the Universal Digital Library

Christian Vandendorpe

Translated from the French by Phyllis Aronoff and Howard Scott

UNIVERSITY OF ILLINOIS PRESS

Urbana and Chicago

Originally published as *Du papyrus à l'hypertexte* by
Les Éditions du Boréal, © 1999 by Éditions du Boréal.

The author thanks the W. D. Jordan Special Collections
Library at Queen's University and the Library of the
University of Ottawa for their kind permission to
reproduce some pages of their incunabula.

Library of Congress Cataloging-in-Publication Data
Vandendorpe, Christian.
From papyrus to hypertext : toward the universal
digital library / Christian Vandendorpe ; translated
from the French by Phyllis Aronoff and Howard Scott.
p.   cm.
Includes bibliographical references and index.
ISBN 978-0-252-03435-0 (cloth : alk. paper) —
ISBN 978-0-252-07625-1 (pbk. : alk. paper)
1. Written communication.
2. Reading.
3. Hypertext systems.
I. Title.
P211.V3613   2009
302.2'244—dc22   2008039601

Contents

Series Preface

Ray Siemens and Susan Schreibman

The application of computational method to the traditional work of the humanities does more than simply accelerate task-oriented work. Helpful as such a gain is, a more important outcome of the combination of computing and the humanities is reaped from the way in which computing has helped change the nature of tasks that can be imagined and performed. Moreover, as our engagement with computing matures, new modes of research become available to us, inviting new research questions, and new research methods and tools, as well as new modes for teaching and publication. Concurrently, expectations about skills have evolved, library purchases have shifted dramatically, and research funding agencies have changed patterns of support.

At the same time as we acknowledge these changes, we must also acknowledge that the very notion of the digital humanities constantly undergoes redefinition of basic principles by a continuous influx of new, vibrant, and diverse communities of practitioners within and well beyond the halls of academe. These practitioners recognize the value that computational method adds to their work, that the computer itself remains an instrument subject to continual innovation, and that collaboration with and competition within many disciplines requires scholars to become and remain current with the advances that can be brought to their work by evolving computational technology.

This series, Topics in the Digital Humanities, is intended to publish works that advance and deepen knowledge and activity in this new and innovative field. The first of these is an English translation of Christian Vandendorpe's *Du papyrus à l'hypertexte: Essai sur les mutations du texte et de la lecture*, as *From Papyrus to Hypertext*. Co-published in 1999 by Boréal Press (Montreal) and La Découverte (Paris), published electronically by oohoo in 2000, and translated into Spanish and published in the series Lengua y estudios literarios (Buenos Aires) as *Del papiro al hipertexto: Ensayo sobre las mutaciones del texto y de la lectura* in 2003, this work has thus already had a significant international impact on digital textual studies.

An intelligent series of short essays on the nature of text as it has been affected by the digital revolution, Vandendorpe's work is truly third-generation, both building on and moving beyond the astonishing specifics of the transformation as it evolved quickly from the 1970s to the end of the 1990s. Thus, Vannevar Bush, Ted Nelson, and others, though very different and spanning a broad period, might be considered part of a continuum of first-generation commentators predicting what is to come; and Espen Aarseth, Michael Joyce, and J. D. Bolter part of a second generation commenting on the details of what is actually coming to pass. Part of what Vandendorpe discusses is very much in this vein, yet it also moves beyond our present engagement with the digital revolution through the philosophical and literary theoretical traditions he engages. His work presents a reflection on the historical, theoretical, and practical position of hypertext as a new medium of communication, situating hypertext in its historical context, offering an inventory of the principal concepts that have informed hypertext theory in the past and will continue to do so in the future, while providing a sort of "dictionnaire raisonné" (encyclopedic dictionary) as it maps the many dimensions of hypertextuality.

While Dr. Vandendorpe's original 1999 argument remains as fresh and essential today as when it first appeared, he has extensively updated this first edition in English to encompass new critical, methodological, and computational methods. This work's great strength is its consideration of the act of reading, especially the relationship between reading technologies and the way in which various technologies affect the reading experiences of a text. In so doing, it shifts focus in scholarly debate from the structure of hypertextual documents to the cognitive process of reading in the electronic environment. In the context of Hans-Georg Gadamer and Mikhail Bakhtin, who have seen the reader's relation to print as always already interactive and dialogistic, Vandendorpe asserts that the reader's response is essential to the meaning of any text. Building his reflection upon Roland Barthes and others, he advances a compelling argument that "stories" naturally unfold in interactive ways; while the Internet might encourage a constant encyclopaedic movement, difficult to understand in terms of traditional narrative, Vandendorpe asserts that narrative is built into the act of reading itself, the path of the reader becoming part of the narrative experience as he or she

Series Preface

Ray Siemens and Susan Schreibman

The application of computational method to the traditional work of the humanities does more than simply accelerate task-oriented work. Helpful as such a gain is, a more important outcome of the combination of computing and the humanities is reaped from the way in which computing has helped change the nature of tasks that can be imagined and performed. Moreover, as our engagement with computing matures, new modes of research become available to us, inviting new research questions, and new research methods and tools, as well as new modes for teaching and publication. Concurrently, expectations about skills have evolved, library purchases have shifted dramatically, and research funding agencies have changed patterns of support.

At the same time as we acknowledge these changes, we must also acknowledge that the very notion of the digital humanities constantly undergoes redefinition of basic principles by a continuous influx of new, vibrant, and diverse communities of practitioners within and well beyond the halls of academe. These practitioners recognize the value that computational method adds to their work, that the computer itself remains an instrument subject to continual innovation, and that collaboration with and competition within many disciplines requires scholars to become and remain current with the advances that can be brought to their work by evolving computational technology.

This series, Topics in the Digital Humanities, is intended to publish works that advance and deepen knowledge and activity in this new and innovative field. The first of these is an English translation of Christian Vandendorpe's *Du papyrus à l'hypertexte: Essai sur les mutations du texte et de la lecture*, as *From Papyrus to Hypertext*. Co-published in 1999 by Boréal Press (Montreal) and La Découverte (Paris), published electronically by oohoo in 2000, and translated into Spanish and published in the series Lengua y estudios literarios (Buenos Aires) as *Del papiro al hipertexto: Ensayo sobre las mutaciones del texto y de la lectura* in 2003, this work has thus already had a significant international impact on digital textual studies.

An intelligent series of short essays on the nature of text as it has been affected by the digital revolution, Vandendorpe's work is truly third-generation, both building on and moving beyond the astonishing specifics of the transformation as it evolved quickly from the 1970s to the end of the 1990s. Thus, Vannevar Bush, Ted Nelson, and others, though very different and spanning a broad period, might be considered part of a continuum of first-generation commentators predicting what is to come; and Espen Aarseth, Michael Joyce, and J. D. Bolter part of a second generation commenting on the details of what is actually coming to pass. Part of what Vandendorpe discusses is very much in this vein, yet it also moves beyond our present engagement with the digital revolution through the philosophical and literary theoretical traditions he engages. His work presents a reflection on the historical, theoretical, and practical position of hypertext as a new medium of communication, situating hypertext in its historical context, offering an inventory of the principal concepts that have informed hypertext theory in the past and will continue to do so in the future, while providing a sort of "dictionnaire raisonné" (encyclopedic dictionary) as it maps the many dimensions of hypertextuality.

While Dr. Vandendorpe's original 1999 argument remains as fresh and essential today as when it first appeared, he has extensively updated this first edition in English to encompass new critical, methodological, and computational methods. This work's great strength is its consideration of the act of reading, especially the relationship between reading technologies and the way in which various technologies affect the reading experiences of a text. In so doing, it shifts focus in scholarly debate from the structure of hypertextual documents to the cognitive process of reading in the electronic environment. In the context of Hans-Georg Gadamer and Mikhail Bakhtin, who have seen the reader's relation to print as always already interactive and dialogistic, Vandendorpe asserts that the reader's response is essential to the meaning of any text. Building his reflection upon Roland Barthes and others, he advances a compelling argument that "stories" naturally unfold in interactive ways; while the Internet might encourage a constant encyclopaedic movement, difficult to understand in terms of traditional narrative, Vandendorpe asserts that narrative is built into the act of reading itself, the path of the reader becoming part of the narrative experience as he or she moves from place to place. His early conclusion that interactivity is no more than "an extension of the reading process" helps us to comprehend the often baffling, and to some disturbing, evolution of textuality in the digital age.

In short, Vandendorpe's work is carefully and intelligently observant of a profound shift in reading behavior. In the tradition of Jerome McGann's *Radiant Textuality*, and Marshall McLuhan's *Gutenberg Galaxy* before it, Vandendorpe's *From Papyrus to Hypertext* presents a most engaging volume to launch this new series.

⠒ ⠒⠒ ⠂
⠂ ⠒⠒ ⠒

For their painstaking efforts in the preparation of this volume, we thank translators Phyllis Aronoff and Howard Scott, and many at the University of Illinois Press, but most especially the director of the press, Willis Regier. For their key contextualization of Vandendorpe's contribution to an important debate of continuing interest to those in the digital humanities, we also thank William Barker, Bertrand Gervais, Ron Tetreault, and William Winder.

From Papyrus to Hypertext

Introduction

Why is this the first chapter? It could just have
well gone somewhere else. In fact, I have to
admit that I wrote Chapter Eight before Chapter
Five, which finally became Chapter Three.

—Charles Nodier, *Moi-même*

Until the late seventies, it was still possible to believe that the effects of computers would be felt only in scientific and technical fields. Today it is clear that computers and the technology associated with them are revolutionizing the ways in which our civilization creates, stores, and transmits knowledge. They will eventually transform the most valuable tool human beings have created to build knowledge and develop their image of themselves and the world: text. And since text exists only in relation to reading, changes in text will have repercussions for reading, just as changes in reading will necessarily lead to the development of other modes of textuality. We do not read hypertext the same way we read a novel, and browsing the Web is a different experience from reading a book or newspaper.

These transformations that affect every aspect of our civilization are the subject of this book, which is one of an increasing number of works situated at the intersection of the history of reading,[1] hypertext,[2] the realm of writing,[3] the "end" of the book, and media studies.[4] This evolution inevitably raises the question of format, or perhaps I should say medium. Should I choose book or hypertext? Although in the final analysis the immaturity of hypertext justifies the use of hard copy for this work, it might seem inconsistent to some to use the old tools to explore a phenomenon as important for our civilization as the digital and hypertext revolution. What would be the value of views that were not backed up by experimentation? Might not the reader suspect the author of bias against the new medium, of waging a rear-guard action or of preaching to the converted? In the interest of intellectual honesty as well as in the spirit of research, most of this book was first written using a hypertext writing tool developed for the purpose, whose functions were refined as the need arose. It was only in the final stage of the writing that the pages created in this way were put into a word-processing program and reworked for print publication. I needed to go through this process in order to experience firsthand the consequences of the choice of medium for the internal organization and even the content of the discussion.

Whereas a book intrinsically has a totalizing function and aims to cover a whole area of knowledge, hypertext encourages the use of a large number of links in order to explore associations between ideas, to "spread out" rather than to "dig," in the hope of engaging readers whose interests are constantly changing, moving from association to association. Every concept referred to in a hypertext is thus potentially a distinct entry that can in turn generate new branchings, or more precisely, new rhizomes. It should be added that hypertext is by nature opaque, unlike a book, which has multiple, constantly accessible reference points. While reading a book is marked by duration and a certain continuity, reading hypertext is marked by a sense of urgency, discontinuity, and constant choices. In fact, every hypertext link challenges the ephemeral contract with the reader: Will the reader click on the hyperlink and continue in his or her quest or abandon the quest?

This reading process necessarily affects the formatting of text, since the writer tends to modulate the discussion according to the attention anticipated. In my case, the transition from hypertext format to book format resulted in a considerable amount of consolidation, greater consistency in the point of view, the elimination of much redundancy, and enunciative changes in the cross-references. All the same, this book is no doubt still strongly marked by the form in which it was conceived. Instead of being organized according to a traditional linear, hierarchical structure, it is presented in the form of blocks of text that may be seen as topics offered for reflection— which makes it more like a collection of essays. The initial hypertext version contained many links between pages, allowing the reader to follow the most appropriate or desired thread of associations. This associative logic had to be abandoned in the paper version, which made the organization of the entries more crucial. Chronological order was not suitable, since most of the topics were not historical in nature. There was no obvious logical order, since there were several intertwining perspectives. Was alphabetical order the solution, then? It has been used for more than eight centuries, in dictionaries for example, to indicate to readers that no order has been imposed on the material. But the sections of this book are not independent of each other. In fact, it was possible to group them according to the themes discussed, among which there is a definite continuity; it is therefore recommended that they be read sequentially.

The reader could certainly also choose to navigate using the index, exploring the more complex entries first. In hypertext, the pages with the most affinities are those that have the largest numbers of hyperlinks to each other. Thus we will see that the entry "tabularity" is the most important. If there is a unifying thread in this book, it is to be found in this concept and its opposite, that of linearity. By spatializing information, tabular text allows the eye to go where it wants and enables the reader to get directly to the point he or she is interested in. This concept is closely related to the concepts of codex and *volumen* and, naturally, to that of hypertext.

This entire book is obviously dominated by the question of reading, which is discussed from various perspectives of meaning and effect, context, readability, cognitive filters, and learned reflexes. How the author conceives of reading in the end determines the format of the text and the degree of control given to the reader or kept by the author. In this respect, the computer has the power to radically change the situation established over millennia of written culture.

One pitfall of my undertaking, which also explains the fragmented form of this book, is the impossibility of categorizing the many potential incarnations of text in a way that embraces their infinite diversity. Over two centuries ago, the authors of Diderot and d'Alembert's *Encyclopédie* attempted to categorize that indefinable object, the book, as follows: "With respect to their qualities, books can be divided into: clear, detailed books, which are of the dogmatic type[;] . . . obscure books, that is, those in which all the words are too generic and are not defined[;] . . . prolix books[;] . . . useful books[;] . . . complete books, which contain everything concerning the subject dealt with. Relatively complete."[5] This classification brings to mind Borges's description of the classification of animals in a Chinese encyclopedia: "These ambiguities, redundancies, and deficiencies recall those attributed by Dr. Franz Kuhn to a certain Chinese encyclopedia entitled *Celestial Emporium of Benevolent Knowledge*. On those remote pages it is written that animals are divided into (a) those that belong to the Emperor, (b) embalmed ones, (c) those that are trained, (d) suckling pigs, (e) mermaids, (f) fabulous ones, (g) stray dogs, (h) those that are included in this classification, (i) those that tremble as if they were mad, (j) innumerable ones, (k) those drawn with a very fine camel's hair brush, (l) others, (m) those that have just broken a flower vase, (n) those that resemble flies from a distance."[6]

It should be noted that the approach presented here is neither classificatory, historical, nor encyclopedic, and especially, that it does not claim to be exhaustive. Its only aim is to offer a reflection on the cultural transformation taking place before our eyes and to attempt to grasp some of the issues involved.

2

In the Beginning Was the Ear

> The fault line between orality and literacy constitutes
> the fundamental plate tectonic in Western expression.
> On the literate side, the neutral theory of commu-
> nication in which "noiseless concepts or ideas" are
> exchanged in a "silent field of mental space." On the
> oral side, ideas exchanged in the emotionally charged
> field of attitude and design, of voice and gesture.
>
> —Richard Lanham, *The Economics of Attention*

For a long time, our experience of literature and our relationship to language took place by way of the ear, which was also our first means of access
to language. For millennia storytellers, bards, and troubadours transmitted
their stories orally to people who came to listen to them. Only much later
did literature free itself from this primary orality, although perhaps never
completely.

A listening situation is defined by three constraints: (a) listeners cannot
determine the time of communication; (b) they do not control the rate of
delivery, but are dependent on the pace chosen by the storyteller; (c) they
cannot backtrack and choose to review content that particularly interests
them, but must follow the thread of the narrative, which is necessarily linear
because it is inscribed in time.

The invention of writing modified this situation by transforming the addressee's relationship to the work. With a written text, readers can always

choose the time of reading and the speed at which they assimilate information. They can also, to a varying extent depending on the type of text, select segments of text—chapters, pages, or paragraphs—and read them in any order they choose. Writing thus allows the reader to escape, in whole or in part, the three fundamental constraints of oral communication. But this liberation did not come about overnight. Long subjected to the standards of oral production, which it strived to replicate, text only gradually distanced itself from them as its material medium was perfected—going from clay tablet to papyrus scroll, and then to the codex or stitched notebook, the ancestor of our book—and as markers were created to facilitate the relationship between writing and reading, making language part of the visual order.

Being situated in the realm of the eye, however, writing lacks the whole intimate dimension conveyed by the voice, with its vibration, its trembling, its hesitations, its silences, its false starts, its repetitions, its tensions. It also deprives the reader of a certain amount of secondary information, because, in addition to being gendered, voices are geographically and socially marked; they reveal the age, culture, education, and psychological attitudes of speakers. A text read out loud thus comes to us laden with all sorts of alluvia related to a specific personality.

Like a fingerprint or a fragment of DNA, every voice is a signature; a text, on the contrary, can be perfectly neutral and devoid of any reference to the person who conceived it. Indeed, this is an ideal that scientific and scholarly writing seems to be increasingly close to achieving, and we will see later why this is so. Writing's intrinsic tendency toward neutrality paradoxically intensifies the quest for style, the individuality of which is highlighted in Buffon's well-known saying, "The style is the man himself." Style is a desperate attempt to restore to the text the signature of the voice as idealized by the writer, and it finds its ultimate justification in the sentence that "reads well," or "sounds good." It is no accident that the concern with style intensified in the second half of the nineteenth century, precisely when the mechanization of printing ensured the predominance of written language. Today, in a strange return to the past, the literary quest for style seems to be increasingly directed toward the rediscovery of orality, as if to compensate for the widening gulf between speech and a type of writing that is more and more mechanized and standardized.

It indeed took a long time before text ceased to be conveyed mainly by the voice. The way of reading that seems normal to us today was not normal for the Greeks or Romans, who saw reading as a way of transmitting text through the voice. In Rome people who were wealthy enough did not read themselves but had specialized slaves read scrolls to them. It was only much later that reading became visual. Thus, around the year 400, Augustine, the Bishop of Hippo Regius, told how he marveled at seeing Ambrose reading with his eyes alone. In his quest for the allegorical meaning of biblical texts, the old scholar had learned to read without moving his lips: "vox autem et lingua quiescebant."[1] It was not until the twelfth century, according to historians of reading, that books were actually designed for silent reading. This necessitated various innovations of a tabular nature to the codex, in particular the change from the continuous writing of the Romans, the *scriptura continua,* to the practice of placing separations between the words, which made its appearance around the seventh century but did not really become common until the ninth century, in monasteries and among scholarly readers.[2]

It was a long time before teaching methods adapted to this revolution. Until about the mid-twentieth century, schools aimed primarily to instill in children the technique of reading out loud. This was reflected among adults in the habit of subvocalization, which experts have criticized for reducing reading speed. While this kind of "oralized" reading was perfectly suited to poetry, which has long been dominated by rhythm and sonority, it was much less suitable for the novel, and it is totally inappropriate for reading newspapers, files, or Web pages.

3

Writing and the Fixation of Thought

"This invention, O king," said Theuth, "will make the Egyptians wiser and will improve their memories; for it is an elixir of memory and wisdom that I have discovered."

—Plato, *Phaedrus,* 274e

Writing was the first great intellectual revolution. It led to what Walter Ong (1982) aptly describes as the "technologizing of the word" and the establishment of a new relationship between language and thought. As long as the experience of language was exclusively oral, reality was never very far behind the words. Exchanges between people took place face to face, and the subjectivity of the language coincided with the communication situation: "I" corresponded to a real person, and "here" and "now" referred to the place and the time of the exchange. The emergence of writing freed communication from the real situation and the details surrounding it: details that the writer became gradually able to render and recreate in words. For a large proportion of exchanges, then, the text would recreate the context.

By fixing thought, writing increased its power and modified its functioning. It introduced the possibility of order, continuity, and consistency where there had been fluidity and chaos. In its natural state, nothing is more unstable than thought; associations are constantly being made and unmade, carried along by new perceptions and the potential of networks of associations. Every minute, new mental constellations may form, as different as the waves breaking on a shore, each one combining the drops of water into a different structure with its own energy. Ephemeral and fluid, thought is as hard to hold on to as smoke, as multifarious and shifting as the light on the sea. Maurice Blanchot expresses this in a fine paradox: "Of thought, it must first of all be said that it is the impossibility of sticking to anything definite—the impossibility, then, of thinking of anything undetermined—and that it is thus the permanent neutralization of all present thought at the same time that it is the repudiation of all absence of thought."[1]

By making it possible to record the traces of a mental configuration and reorganize them at will, writing introduced a new order in the history of humanity. Through writing, thoughts can be refined and reworked repeatedly, can undergo controlled modifications and unlimited expansion, without the repetition that characterizes oral transmission. What was fluid and moving can become as precise and organized as crystal, and confusion can give way to system. In short, through writing, the productions of the mind enter the objective order of the visible.

Writing changed not only the relationship of individuals to their own thoughts, but also their relationship to the thoughts of others as they are objectified in the text, thoughts under whose rule one temporarily agrees to place oneself when one begins to read.

4

The Power of the Written Sign

As Jean Molino notes, "A text inscribes only what is important. It has a specific relationship to the truth."[1] In the human imagination and the memory of cultures, writing is invested with formidable symbolic value. Among the Assyrians and Babylonians, scribes were an aristocratic caste that claimed to see "the writing of heaven" in the pattern of the stars. According to the ancient Egyptians, writing was created and given to humanity by the god Thoth. The word *hieroglyph* means "sacred writing," and the scribe's pen was also the symbol for truth.[2] In Hebrew culture, the book, as the repository of the word of God, is considered sacred.

The classical Greeks did not have a caste responsible for preserving the secret of writing and were thus less inclined to regard the book as sacred. Plato was critical of writing and concerned about the changes it would bring to traditional culture. Seeing it as an extension of individual and social memory, he sensed that it would transform the way tradition was transmitted. It is undoubtedly because of his attachment to the oral tradition, which was still strong in his master Socrates, that he wrote most of his works in the form of dialogues: "For Socrates, written texts were nothing more than an adjunct to memory for those who were already familiar with the content, but they could never provide wisdom; that was the privilege of oral discourse."[3]

Nor did ancient Rome hold the book in high esteem. But the situation changed radically with the advent of Christianity. Perhaps as a result of its Jewish roots, the Christian religion was deeply imbued with the idea of the book and writing, and was the source of the dissemination of the codex. From the early centuries of the Common Era, representations of the book had a special place in Christianity, so much so that it has been described as a religion of the book.[4] Born of this dual Judeo-Christian source, respect for the book was long maintained in our culture. It reached its culmination with the poet Stéphane Mallarmé, who was extremely sensitive to the visual space of the book and for whom "all earthy existence must ultimately be contained in a book."[5] The same exaltation of the book is found in writers in the Jewish tradition, such as Edmond Jabès.

One might hypothesize that the extraordinary prestige of writing, which goes beyond the mere functional aspects of this major invention, is based on the fact that reading text combines two major senses: sight, the highest sense, and hearing, the sense associated with our first experience of the world and in particular of the raw material of language. These two means of perceiving external data have long been combined in the act of reading—at least as long as it was accompanied by vocalization or subvocalization. And the fruitful combination that occurs in the reader's mind tends to give text the seal of truth, with vocalization providing confirmation for what was first perceived by the eye, and vice versa.

5

Writing and Orality

The interiorization of the technology of the
phonetic alphabet translates man from the magical
world of the ear to the neutral visual world.
—Marshall McLuhan, *The Gutenberg Galaxy*

For a long time, writing was seen as a pure transcription of speech—or at best a "supplement" to speech. This classic position was expressed by Rousseau in *Émile:* "Languages are made to be spoken, writing serves only as a supplement to speech; if there are some languages that are only written, and that one cannot speak, belonging only to the sciences, it would be of no use in civil life."[1] Far from breaking with this position, modern linguistics as founded by Saussure made the primacy of oral language a basic methodological principle: "Language and writing are two distinct systems of signs; the second exists for the sole purpose of representing the first. The linguistic object is not both the written and spoken forms of words; the spoken forms alone constitute the object. But the spoken word is so intimately bound to its written image that the latter manages to usurp the main role. People attach even more importance to the written image of a vocal sign than to the sign itself. A similar mistake would be in thinking that more can be learned about someone by looking at his photograph than by viewing him directly."[2]

Derrida attacks these "traditional" positions head-on, advocating a grammatology in which writing would be invested with an authority and a legitimacy equal to those of oral language. In this debate, both parties can justly claim to represent modernity. On the one hand, linguistics had to overcome the contempt generally felt by literate people for primary orality, which goes back in individual experience to memories of early childhood. By adopting a rigorous methodological foundation, the discipline was able to establish itself as a science and obtain remarkable results, particularly in the field of phonology. On the other hand, Louis Hjelmslev's concept of written language as an autonomous code is also modern and is based in part on developments in semiotics and, historically, on the slow process through which text and reading freed themselves from their ancient matrix of orality.

There is little doubt today that a written language can function without reference to an oral mother tongue learned in early childhood. Nevertheless, although the socially valued form of reading tends to avoid oralization, the relationship between ocular and phonological mechanisms is more mysterious than ever. While in the eighties reading was considered a purely visual phenomenon, independent of the voice, recent psychological studies seem to indicate that orality is still present in the cerebral mechanisms involved in reading, and that phonological codes are activated as soon as the eyes focus on a text.[3]

Without trying to resolve the question of primacy in favor of either the oral or the written code, let us briefly review the main differences. Oral discourse takes place in an irreversible temporal linear flow. The listener thus cannot move from one section of a discourse to another, cannot fast-forward through it, pausing at the key points or finding a particular sentence. Even with modern recording technology, oral language is still essentially a prisoner of the temporal thread, placing the listener in a position of dependency on it. This situation has many consequences.

Studies in cultural anthropology, such as that of Walter Ong, have shown that oral societies share certain characteristics with regard to the use of language. The most important of these, one that has been observed in all studies of oral literature, is a marked preference for stereotyped expressions and formulas: "oral cultures not only express themselves in formulas, but also think in formulas."[4] This trait is probably the one that is most foreign to our modern conception of literary language, which since the romantic revolution has been associated with originality. Jean Paulhan's study of hainteny—improvised poems recited by two competitors in poetic contests in traditional Malagasy society—showed that the very purpose of this activity was the knowledge and celebration of expressions and formulas. The use in the Icelandic sagas circa 1000 of large numbers of kennings—fixed metaphors such as "storm of swords" for "battle" and "food for crows" for "corpse"—may be attributed to this same taste for formulas. These poetry games, which are enigmatic to those of us who do not belong to the interpretive communities for which they were intended, were described by Borges as "one of the coldest aberrations recorded in histories of literature."[5]

The formulaic aspect also has consequences for the choice of themes, which are limited to a basic set of recurring standardized situations. This thematic poverty goes hand-in-hand with the tendency to favor profusion over conciseness and to use fixed attributes to identify characters or phenomena. At a deeper level, some anthropologists feel that the situation of primary orality of primitive societies also had consequences for thinking itself, and that when a system of writing conventions becomes widely available in a society, a new mind-set and a new relation to knowledge take hold. In a persuasive series of essays on writing, the anthropologist Jack Goody has shown that writing extends the field of rationality, encourages skepticism, and develops logical thinking.

Independently of the type of society or the period, an examination of oral utterances shows that there is considerable tolerance for problems of structure and organization of discourse. Thematic drift is almost inevitable because a speaker is often unable to resist the attraction of a new train of thought that emerges through association with what he or she is saying. In addition, oral discourse leaves unspoken a great deal of information related to the situation and the overall context, since the speakers are in each other's presence and can usually manage with an implicit reference to the shared situation. While spontaneous oral discourse thus inevitably bears the scars resulting from its production under conditions of urgency, written language is the idealized face of language, the place where it can pretend to perfection.

6

Standards of Readability

A history of literature could be written in terms
of the ways in which audiences have successively
been fictionalized from the time when writing
broke away from oral performance.
—Walter Ong, *Interfaces of the Word*

A complex set of standards of readability, developed over the centuries, have made text more legible and more effective. These standards were not issued by a single authority, but are the result of practices and rules established by the many actors that participate in the production of a text, from author to bookseller, including reading and editorial committees, publisher, editor, book designer, printer, juries for literary prizes, critics, and of course readers.

The first of these standards is that of the visual uniformity of a body of text. This requirement, which was already present in ancient steles and papyruses, was reaffirmed at the end of a period of great barbarism, when Alcuin, at the invitation of Charlemagne, established the superb cursive handwriting known as Carolingian minuscule in the *scriptoria*, or copyists' workshops, of monasteries. Through tested and logically organized procedures, the writing of the professional scribes achieved a surprising degree of uniformity. However, it was the introduction of printing around 1450 that made it possible to ensure absolute regularity, over hundreds of pages, in the size of the letters, the spacing between words and between lines, and justification, thus raising the presentation of text to mechanical perfection. Writing a century after this invention, Rabelais still expresses admiration for the new medium: "Printing likewise is now in use, so elegant and so correct that better cannot be imagined, although it was found out but in my time by divine inspiration."[1]

All these features have more than a mere ornamental function; their purpose is to ensure the uniformity of the visual material so as to facilitate the act of reading, allowing it to be consigned largely to automatic cognitive processes and preventing interference. Typography of high quality is thus the reader's first ally. It also makes books more pleasant to read, and creates an impression conducive to reception of the message. Format also plays a role, and in order to define paper formats with harmonious proportions, printers are said to have used the golden ratio, an irrational number roughly equivalent to the ratio 5 : 8, which Leonardo da Vinci called the golden section (cf. Robert Bringhurst).

Over the centuries, there developed in publishing a semiotics of the text as object, which left no aspect of the book to chance. Conflicts occur, of course, between the demands of layout and economic constraints, as shown in the tendency to reduce the size of margins in mass-market publishing. Books with wide margins, like those commonly published in the eighteenth and early nineteenth centuries, provide reading comfort unmatched in a more crowded layout in which the text cannot "breathe." To prevent confusion between the column of text and neighboring elements, the two-column layout, which was often felt to be too dense and crowded, was abandoned in books, although on a wide enough page short lines of text are easier to read than longer ones. Although writers were generally excluded from decisions on the presentation of their texts, there were some, such as La Fontaine and Mallarmé, who paid a great deal of attention to it. The eminent typographer and publisher Charles Peignot reported that "Paul Valéry looked at the type, judging how readable the letters were and considering whether their design created a climate favorable to his message."[2]

The same desire for optimal readability led to the standardization of spelling, for which printers gradually came to assume responsibility as they developed a collective awareness of the reading process. According to McLuhan, "Print altered not only the spelling and grammar but the accentuation and inflexion of languages, and made 'bad grammar' possible."[3] As late as the early seventeenth century, the idea of a single way to spell a word had not yet taken hold. During that century, debate became more and more vigorous between advocates of spelling that was as close as possible to pronunciation and those favoring spelling that incorporated traces of morphology, history, and etymology—even if the latter were sometimes debatable or even totally erroneous. Living in an age when spelling has long been standardized, we today can hardly imagine how much graphemic variations slowed down reading and kept it subordinated to orality. Indeed, it was only the habit of reading orally that made it possible for readers to recognize the same semantic content in different spellings. Contemporary readers have this kind of experience only when faced with irregular spellings or deliberate cacography.

Since variations in spelling slowed reading and hampered the spread of written language, it is hardly surprising that it was printers who finally took the lead in applying standards in this area and that their style conventions with regard to capital letters, abbreviations, and other details became a model of precision and indeed the ultimate standard with regard to spelling. In the English-speaking world, major newspapers and publishing firms, with their style manuals, imposed uniform spelling in given geographic areas. Even in France, the decrees of the Académie française were not heeded when they conflicted with those of the powerful book and publishing organizations.

The debate over punctuation was not as lively as the one over spelling, and responsibility for it was given to printers quite early. This is undoubtedly why, even in a critical edition, it is usually considered legitimate to change the punctuation of an old text in accordance with current standards. One need only compare recent editions of seventeenth- or eighteenth-century texts with the originals to see how much the dialogue gains in readability by being presented in the modern way, using indents or quotation marks for the words of the speakers.

Standards of readability also have obvious effects on syntax, resulting in changes that, far from being dictated by the arbitrary decisions of grammarians, are designed to make constructions as unequivocal as possible. A good example is the prohibition of the dangling participle, as in the sentence "Being completely broke, his banker refused to give him any more loans." According to the rules of standard English, a participle at the beginning of a sentence is assumed to be connected to the subject of the principal clause. This rule has the advantage of preventing any hesitation on the part of readers when they encounter a participle at the beginning of a sentence, and enables them to construct the meaning as the words are processed, without any delay. Every microsecond thus gained translates into greater efficiency for the reader.

The same trend toward the elimination of ambiguity can be seen in textual grammar. Although, as Roman Jakobson has shown, the freedom of the speaker increases as one rises in the hierarchy of linguistic manifestations, the text is not a space of absolute freedom. Various textual constraints, which are dictated by respect for readers and a desire to facilitate their work, have gradually been imposed on writers. An example is the rule that in a narrative in the third person, all deictic elements—terms referring to the situation of an utterance, such as "yesterday," "tomorrow," and "here"—must be changed to their co-textual equivalents—"the day before," "the next day," and "there." This transposition, which emerged relatively recently, is not gratuitous, since it protects the reader from the risk, however minimal, of confusing a reference to the space or time of the text with one related to the space or time of the reading.

The refinement of writing conventions over the centuries also involved the erasure of any references to the person of the author and the adoption of an instance of historical utterance stripped of all traces of the subjectivity characteristic of oral discourse. "I" and "me" thus gave way either to "we" and "us," which may sometimes include the reader, or to various impersonal strategies of utterance, at least in informational and scientific writing. This trend existed long before Pascal's aphorism "Le moi est haïssable" ["The I is hateful"] denounced the naïve tendency of the "I" to immediately place itself at the center of its discourse. In fact, the Greek historian Dionysius of Halicarnassus was already very conscious of the imperative of objectivity, as shown by the beginning of his *Antiquities of Rome*, written in the first century BCE: "Although it is much against my will to indulge in the explanatory statements usually given in the prefaces to histories, yet I am obliged to prefix to this work some remarks concerning myself. In doing this it is neither my intention to dwell too long on my own praise, which I know would be distasteful to the reader."[4]

The trend toward impersonal utterance was not based on moral principles; rather, it arose from a writing strategy that aimed to make the text a neutral space free of any subjective filter that could get in the way of the reader's total involvement. It is as if the ideal of the text was implicitly to be an autonomous utterance in which no one is speaking to anyone. The reading mind clearly functions best when the text is devoid of any trace of subjectivity and completely detached from its author. The text can thus be more easily examined from the outside and readers will not feel the gaze of the other, whose effect can be as paralyzing as that of the Medusa. By excluding effects and emotions, the neutrality of the text facilitates its appropriation by the intellect. There is a clear parallel with the well-known phenomenon of averting one's gaze when carrying out a task involving remembering: psychologists see this gaze turned obliquely upward as intended to neutralize cognitive pressure from the environment and ensure maximum concentration. Similarly, once stripped of the subjectivity inherent in physical interactions, the text can become the site where the reader exercises intellectual concentration without hindrance or psychological pressure of any kind; the data will then be directly accessible to the intellect as pure semiotic material, without interference from the emotions. With the spread of printing, this neutrality was increasingly perceived as a fundamental characteristic of written language and was reinforced by the simplicity of the layout.

For the same reason, scientific and informational texts avoid addressing the reader directly, since the use of "you" demands a degree of involvement the addressee is not always willing to grant except in correspondence. The same is true of administrative texts. For example, a sign saying "Do not smoke" addresses the reader much more insistently than one that simply says "No smoking." Overly direct remarks are known to be much more likely to provoke a hostile response than impersonal formulations. Nominalization, as we see in the above example, helps to eliminate these traces of subjectivity. It also has the effect of reinforcing the features that mark discourse as written, increasing its distance from oral discourse. In this sense, it is a marker of textuality, highlighting the work of writing. Scientific and scholarly prose have a particular affinity for this mode of expression because it communicates a maximum amount of information very succinctly. This is the normal mode of expression of an encyclopedia article: "The gravitational attraction between the Earth and the Moon causes the tides on Earth. The same effect on the Moon has led to its tidal locking" (Wikipedia, "Earth"). Although nominalization is not acceptable in oral language because of the density of expression it entails, it opens up many stylistic possibilities, in particular when a thematic thread is carried from one sentence to the next. But it results in a high degree of abstraction and thus can easily give rise to the type of impenetrable jargon modern technocrats hide behind. It is a practice that should be used in very small doses, and its handling requires that the writer have an acute awareness of the readers being addressed.

For its deliberate play with ambiguity, hyperbole, and ornate expressions, rhetoric was long ago barred from scientific texts. In the English-speaking world, its banishment was explicitly proclaimed in 1666 by the Royal Society of London.[5] As studies have shown, there is no reason to pile on rhetorical flourishes if they have a negative effect on the speed of reading.[6] In addition, rhetorical flourishes introduce an emotional dimension that hinders the reader's concentration on the subject at hand. For these reasons, the only rhetorical devices that are still used in scholarly texts are those that, like parallelism and antithesis, facilitate the reader's task by reinforcing the

symmetry of the information presented. Similarly, sudden variations in levels of language are carefully avoided, because they create a rhetorical effect
and tend to establish an atmosphere of familiarity and emotion that may be
perceived as inappropriate.

Finally, the need for readability also gives rise to a demand for coherence,
requiring that every element of a text should be pertinent to the central
theme and that potential disparities among various points of view should be
smoothed over by connectives or transitions. Unlike oral language, which
readily jumps from one thing to another, text is supposed to be centered
on a single axis, as recommended by Julien Benda: "To me, making a book
consists essentially of getting hold of a main idea, in relation to which all
kinds of ideas I have been jotting down for a long time will begin to become
organized in a certain direction. . . . Once I have that, I write it on my table
so as to always have it in front of my eyes; from then on, I do not write a line
without confronting it with this idea and seeing if it is related to it."[7]

Anne-Marie Christin attributes our difficulty with thinking the ambiguous, the vague, and the unresolved to the logocentrism that results from
alphabetical writing.[8] She contrasts our tradition with that of the people of
Easter Island, for whom the purpose of writing is to "revive an active duality
between the gaze and the word, to spark a creative transfer between them."[9]
We may deplore the fact that, in our tradition, writing has sought to bring
into text all the elements that make it a site of significations that is autonomous and independent of the external context. But we have to recognize
that this rejection of the unresolved is precisely a condition for the optimal
functioning of the "textual machine," whose driving force is its linearity.

The increase in constraints designed to eliminate all ambiguity from text
admittedly facilitates reading, making it faster and more efficient. Reading
can also be assisted by computerized aids, which have become necessary as a
result of the growing volume of information to be managed every day; these
include Web search tools and text analysis tools currently being developed,
notably at portal.tapor.ca. We need to recognize, however, that the relationship between reading and writing is a zero-sum game, in which the gains of
the former come at the cost of more constraints for the latter. Thus the activity of writing, which was already extremely complex, becomes even more so,
especially if the author wants to produce texts that can be read by an increasingly broad and distant readership and processed by the above-mentioned
programs or even translated automatically. In a society that is increasingly
information-based, the movement toward neutrality and objectivity that

has been under way since the spread of print will necessarily be reinforced, especially in scientific texts.

As we have seen, codes of readability invariably tend to accentuate the separation between written and oral language. In the major languages of communication, the situation has reached a point where literature, which was long confined to the most standardized written forms, is moving toward casual everyday oral language. We can surely see in this a desire by some writers to narrow the gap between the two major modes of linguistic expression, oral and written, by exploiting the language that was learned first by every speaking being and that will thus always be felt to be the rawest, "truest," and richest in emotion.

7

Linearity and Tabularity

It is generally agreed that reading is a linear process, and that readers pick up cues as they follow a text line by line. If we look at this process more closely, however, it becomes clear that there are many activities involved in reading a book to which the concept of linearity does not apply. Linearity designates a series of elements that follow each other in an inviolable or preestablished order. Best exemplified by the succession of hours or days, it belongs essentially to the realm of time, but also applies to two-dimensional space, i.e., points on a straight line. This concept contrasts with that of tabularity, in which readers can visually access data in the order they choose, identifying sections of interest beforehand, in much the same way as when looking at a painting the eye may contemplate any part.

Philosophically, linearity, the dominant way of thinking for centuries, came into conflict with powerful trends in early twentieth-century physics, a discipline marked by the desire to eliminate time. For Albert Einstein, time was only an illusion masking the immutability of the fundamental laws. Linearity is also intimately connected with the concepts of authority and constraint: it implies the obligation to follow a certain number of steps in a prescribed order. For this reason, linearity can easily be perceived as an intolerable limitation on the sovereign freedom of the individual. It therefore comes as no surprise that it became the whipping boy for modernity.

Because words are necessarily read in sequence, the book is almost inevitably associated with linearity—which is certainly true for the novel. According to Derrida, "the end of linear writing is indeed the end of the book, even if, even today, it is within the form of a book that new writings—literary or theoretical—allow themselves to be, for better or for worse, encased."[1]

But if books are to be considered linear, then what about speech, which inevitably occurs over a span of time, since the words must be perceived one after the other by the listener? And linearity has a cost: the frustration one may feel at having to listen to the news on the radio in an order that is not of one's own choosing, for example, or having to pick up voicemail messages in chronological order when one lacks sophisticated tools for managing voicemail. But written language allows us at least partially to escape linearity, since the eye can take in a page in a glance or can settle successively on various points chosen according to different criteria. Once segmented into coherent blocks of information, a text forms a mosaic that readers can approach as they wish. In the form of the codex, which permits an elaborate use of space, the book acquired many elements of tabularity, which contributed to changes in the nature of text and of language itself, as is shown by the gap that developed between written and spoken language. Any discussion of linearity that fails to take into account this necessary distinction between written and oral language will not get very far. We will therefore examine the concepts of linearity and tabularity in terms of *content*, the *language material*, and in another section, the *medium*.

A narrative that follows a strict chronological order is an example of linearity of content, at least with respect to events. If such a narrative is presented orally, the linearity of the content will coincide with the linearity of the medium. But in written form, it can be arranged in a medium that is more or less linear, ranging from the *volumen* or papyrus scroll used in ancient Greece and Rome, for example, to the newspaper page, in which the paragraphs are preceded by headings highlighting various information, so that readers can select and read them in the order that interests them—in other words, in a nonlinear fashion.

In terms of thematic and symbolic content, texts are often far from linear. In fact, the term *text* itself, which comes from the Latin *textus*, originally referred to the action of weaving, intertwining, or braiding, which implies the existence of several threads in a web and the creation of patterns through the periodic reappearance of these threads. Thus the visual metaphor has been present in the very concept of text from the earliest times. This paradigmatic aspect of text belongs to the spatial order. The process of generating meaning while reading is not necessarily linear, and semioticians such as A. J. Greimas and J. Courtés have shown that "the existence of pluri-isotopic texts contradicts the linearity of signification at the level of the content."[2]

Second, the language material may also be linear to a greater or lesser degree. Whatever interferes with reading or listening, whatever interrupts the thread of the text, is likely to come from the deliberate use of what might be called the tabularity of the language material, insofar as this material shows regularities. Anne-Marie Christin notes that among the Dogon, the metaphor of weaving is applied to speech, which is seen as the verbal fabric of the group.[3] Similarly, poetry may be given a "tabular reading," as discussed by Groupe μ, who examined the use of rhythm, sonorities, parallelisms, and isotopies in the poetic text. These elements might be seen as a form of tabularity if that concept were not essentially associated with sight. To avoid any confusion, one should speak here of "auditory tabularity," which is manifested in meter and assonances or rhyme. This kind of tabularity undoubtedly goes back to a very ancient time, when the transmission of human experience depended wholly on the voice.

The tabular formatting of sound material expresses the same purpose and has the same function as visual tabularity: to provide listeners with sound patterns that will help them mentally process the data by giving these data a mnemonic resonance. As Walter J. Ong, who specialized in the study of oral culture, aptly stated: "In a primary oral culture, to solve effectively the problem of retaining and retrieving carefully articulated thought, you have to do your thinking in mnemonic patterns, shaped for ready oral recurrence. Your thought must come into being in heavily rhythmic, balanced patterns, in repetitions or antitheses, in alliterations and assonances, in epithetic and other formulary expressions, in standard thematic settings . . ., in proverbs."[4] Let us recall, for example, that ancient Greek poetry had developed extremely sophisticated metrics, which took into account the lengths of syllables as well as the tonic accent. It had also developed specialized types of meters for various poetic genres. These extremely constraining sound patterns helped the itinerant bards to remember thousands of verses. Even today, the structure of sayings and proverbs—"A friend in need is a friend indeed," "No pain, no gain"—shows this close affinity between meaning structure and sound structure, with the former being based on the latter in order to facilitate memorization and produce a truth effect.

As long as poetry was dependent on speech, sound remained dominant. But when print extended its sway, heralding the triumph of visual tabularity over the auditory domain, poets such as Paul Verlaine rebelled against the dictatorship of meter. Poetry then took new directions, with Stéphane Mallarmé maintaining that the mystery of the poem lay not only in sonorities, but that the written medium must also play a role: "Yes, I know; Mystery is said to be Music's domain. But the written word also lays claim to it."[5] In "Un coup de dés" ("A Roll of the Dice"), he sought to write a poem that could be scanned visually, using the size of the characters and the arrangement of the words on the page, thus initiating a movement of experimental typography.

Although this movement came up against the limits imposed by our modes of perception,[6] a new paradigm was established in which the material indication of poetic language is the arrangement of the text on the whiteness of the page rather than conformity to a code of versification. But sonorities still play an important role in songs and certain specialized languages, such as political discourse and advertising. Where there is an obvious interest in creating a lasting memory of the message, auditory tabularity—e.g., "I like Ike"—continues to be much sought after.

Linearity and tabularity are closely dependent on the kind of text and the type of work. The encyclopedia and the dictionary, quintessential reference works, do not call for linear reading, insofar as that involves reading from the first page to the last. In this type of text, which functions implicitly on the semidialogic model of the question and answer, the context is not created very elaborately, since it is already present in the need to consult of the reader formulating the question.

In the case of an epic or a novel, on the other hand, the mode of apprehension normally expected by the reader is undeniably linear and continuous. At first glance, the narrative is the prototype of a linear verbal mass with little or no tabularity. To tell a story means essentially to unwind a temporal thread: a narrative exists as soon as a given situation can be linked to a previous state and related to a succession of events and actions. To stimulate interest and suspense, the story is most often told in order from beginning to end (without precluding the possibility of prolepsis or analepsis), since this order allows the reader or listener to clearly grasp the order of events and the narrative links. In most stories told by children, only two or three connectives—"then," "and," "so"—are used to mark how actions are related. Some contemporary narratives are not divided into chapters or paragraphs, so that the reader has no choice but to follow the thread of the text from the first page to the last.

In favor of linearity, it should be recalled that it makes reading highly automatic. Since each sentence provides context for understanding the following one, readers have only to let themselves be carried along by the thread of the text in order to produce meaning. In reading highly tabular texts, and aphorisms or fragments in general, the automatic reflexes of reading may become less effective and play a lesser role, because of the fact that the context for understanding has to be recreated by the reader for every new block of text.

In the case of canonical narratives, the resonance of the linear thread is such that the paradigmatic aspects have become evident only relatively recently, with the appearance of structural studies by Vladimir Propp, Roland Barthes, A. J. Greimas, and others. Although these works at first had little influence on the writing of novels, there have since been increasing numbers of books that lend themselves to a tabular reading process, or even encourage or require it. This is the case, for example, for *Life: A User's Manual*, by Georges Perec, in which a very detailed index allows readers, if they wish, to read in sequence all the chapters in which a particular character appears. *Pale Fire*, by Vladimir Nabokov, invites readers to make all the connections possible between an introduction written by a fictitious character, a 999–line poem in four cantos, a commentary on the poem, and an index. *Dictionary of the Khazars*, by Milorad Pavić, offers an extreme example of a tabular narrative, in which the elements are organized in the form of dictionary entries, in alphabetical order. And when speaking of tabular narrative, one must obviously cite its masters, Italo Calvino and Julio Cortázar, as well as their common ancestor, Laurence Sterne, author of the extraordinary *Life and Opinions of Tristram Shandy, Gentleman* (1760).

Although the canonical narrative is quite far removed from a hypertext structure, one should not conclude that it is totally linear. Many writers do indeed provide a constraining sequential thread that necessitates reading a book from beginning to end. But in so doing, they also aim to create a nonlinear structure in the reader's mind and to force the reader to carry out operations of reorganization that are sometimes very complex, as is the case in works as varied as Balzac's "Sarrasine," Proust's *À la recherche du temps perdu* [*Remembrance of Things Past* or *In Search of Lost Time*], and Garcia Marquez's *Chronicle of a Death Foretold*. According to Georg Lukács, "one can almost say that the whole inner action of a novel is nothing else but a struggle against the power of time."[7] It is precisely because the basic fabric of the narrative is time that the time of the narrative rarely coincides with the time of history. From the *Iliad* on, the literary narrative has distinguished itself from the folk narrative by beginning *in medias res*. Since then, the novel has explored most uses of achronia that could be invented, as is shown by Gérard Genette in his works on narratology.

But other elements come into play in a novel. Going beyond the old metaphor of the fabric, Proust conceived of his work as a cathedral, a three-dimensional space in which all the elements were organically linked and associated through complex symbolisms. Any writer aims essentially to create in the reader's mind a web of associations among dozens, or even thousands, of elements—hypertext *avant la lettre*. As Roland Barthes pointed out, "The classic text, therefore, is actually tabular (and not linear), but its tabularity is vectorized, it follows a logical-temporal order."[8] This internal tabularity has become more pronounced in works by many contemporary writers, who juxtapose the stories of various characters and alternate competing narrative threads constructed so as to periodically bring in certain elements. Sometimes, the change from one thread to another occurs with a minimum of transition, abruptly forcing the reader to reorganize the context.

In this quest for an increasingly emphatic and obvious tabularity, the modern novel has tended to borrow its methods of composition from painting. As Claude Simon observed in an interview with Philippe Sollers: "[Once] the novel is no longer considered a means of instruction, social instruction as in the case of Balzac, a didactic text, . . . methods of composition emerge that are those of painting, music, or architecture: repetition of a particular element, variations, associations, oppositions, contrasts, etc. Or, as in mathematics, arrangements, permutations, combinations."[9] Elsewhere, Simon showed how he used color references to order a series of narrative tableaux in *La Route des Flandres* [*The Flanders Road*] in order to produce a cyclical effect.[10] It must be recognized that such effects would be destroyed if the paragraphs were read in random order—just as a Bach suite would lose its essential beauty if it were played in random sequences of notes through the clicks of a mouse. Even in the visual realm, in which syntax is very lax, a painting cannot be reduced to a conglomeration of basic elements provided by the creator to be arranged by the viewer.

In spite of strong trends toward freedom for the reader and toward the use of hypertext techniques, we cannot simply dismiss the concept of a work of art as a whole that is more than the sum of its parts, which was already one of Aristotle's criteria of tragedy: "Now, according to our definition Tragedy is an imitation of an action that is complete, and whole, and of a certain magnitude; for there may be a whole that is wanting in magnitude. A whole is that which has a beginning, a middle, and an end. . . . A well constructed plot, therefore, must neither begin nor end at haphazard, but conform to these principles."[11] If the narrative of linear content has been so successful until now, it is because it implicitly promises a maximum of meaning for readers who follow the thread of the text: We learn very young that being given the solution to a mystery before reading the book is a sure way to spoil our fun.

It should be noted, furthermore, that while a novel on paper is far from being automatically linear, a hypertext is not necessarily nonlinear. The pages or segments may be rigorously sequential, forcing the reader to read them in a fixed order, one even more fixed than that of the pages of a book, because it is always possible to open a book to any page one wishes while a hypertext can be programmed to totally control the reader's path. This said, hypertext by nature lends itself ideally to a variety of reading paths and to multisequential navigation. In the light of what can be done with these media, it no longer seems possible to maintain the dichotomy between linear and nonlinear media, and more and more theorists now reject this distinction.[12]

8

Toward the Tabular Text

Unlike hieroglyphic writing, whose pictographic component gives it a visual, spectacular aspect, alphabetic writing was conceived as a transcription of speech and was from its inception associated with the linearity of orality. This linearity is aptly symbolized in the arrangement used in early Greek writing, in which the characters in the first line were aligned from left to right, and those in the next line, from right to left, with the characters sometimes inverted, imitating the path of a plow working a field, a metaphor that gave this type of writing its name: *boustrophedon*.[1] Readers were supposed to follow with their eyes the uninterrupted movement the hand of the scribe had traced.

Orality thus extended its influence over the medium of text. The scribe lined up columns of text on sheets of papyrus—which had been in use since 3000 BCE—until he came to the end of the scroll. Despite the characteristics that made the papyrus scroll the quintessential book for three millennia, the fact that it was rolled up into a *volumen* placed serious limitations on the expansion of writing and helped maintain the book's dependence on oral language. It was taken for granted that readers would read from the first line to the last and that they had no choice but to immerse themselves in the text, unrolling the *volumen* as a storyteller recounts a story in a strictly linear continuous order. In addition, readers needed both hands to unroll the papyrus, which made it impossible to take notes or annotate the text. Worse still, as Martial observed, readers would often have to use their chin when rerolling the *volumen*, leaving marks on the edge that were rather off-putting to other library users ("Sic noua nec mento sordida charta iuuat" ["How pleasant is a new exemplar unsoiled by chins"].[2]

The advent of the codex was a radical break with this old order, and it brought about a revolution in the reader's relationship to the text. A codex consists of pages folded and bound to form what we today call a book. These pages were made of papyrus or parchment—paper having appeared in Europe only in the 1100s. The codex emerged in classical Rome, several decades before the Common Era, at the time of Horace, who used one himself as a notebook. Smaller and easier to handle than a scroll, the codex was also more economical, because it allowed scribes to write on both sides and even to scrape off the surface and write on it again. But because of its antiquity, the scroll was still considered to have greater dignity and was preferred by the cultured elite, a status the codex did not acquire for several centuries. The transition really took place only in the fourth century in the Roman Empire. And it took even longer for the new medium to free itself from the model of the *volumen*—just as it took the automobile several decades to completely rid itself of the model of the horse-drawn carriage. Such is the inertia of dominant cultural representations.

Christians were the first to adopt the codex, which they used to spread the Gospels. The new format, which was smaller, more compact, and easier to hide and to handle than the scroll, also had the advantage of representing a sharp break with the tradition of the Jewish Bible. Historians find more and more evidence that the latter reason was in part responsible for the choice of the codex format by the Christians, but the wide adoption of the codex over the following centuries was essentially due to "the twin advantages of comprehensiveness and convenience."[3]

The new element the codex introduced into the economy of the book was the page. I will look at the problem of the integration of this important innovation into the digital order in the section "The End of the Page? [chapter 34]" It was the page that made it possible for text to break away from the continuity and linearity of the scroll and allowed it to be much more easily manipulated. Over the course of a slow but irreversible evolution, the page made text part of the tabular order.

The codex is the quintessential book, without which the pursuit and dissemination of knowledge in our civilization could not have developed as fully as they have. The codex gave rise to a new relationship between reader and text. As one historian of the book writes, "This was a crucial development in the history of the book, perhaps even more important than that brought about by Gutenberg, because it modified the form of the book and required readers to completely change their physical position."[4] The codex left one of the reader's hands free, allowing him or her to take part in the cycle of writing by making annotations, thus becoming more than a mere recipient of the text. Readers could also now access the text directly at any point. A bookmark let them take up reading where they left off, further altering their relationship to the text. As another historian notes, it took "twenty centuries for us to realize that the fundamental importance of the codex for our civilization was to enable selective, noncontinuous reading, thus contributing to the development of mental structures in which the text is dissociated from speech and its rhythms."[5]

When the potential of this union of form and content in the page became apparent, various types of visual markers were gradually added to the organization of the book to help readers find their bearings more easily in the mass of text and make reading easier and more efficient. Since the page constitutes a visual unit of information related to the preceding and the following pages, allowing it to be numbered and given a header, it has an autonomy that the column of text in the *volumen* did not. Thanks to the page, it is possible to leaf through a book and quickly know its contents, or at least the essentials.

The page can be displayed for all to see, inviting monks in scriptoria to combine text and images. While the papyrus was rolled up again after reading, the codex can remain open to a double page, as demonstrated by the big psalters of the Middle Ages that were displayed on their lecterns in churches. The page was thus the place where the text, which was previously seen as a mere transcription of the voice, entered the visual order. From then on, it would increasingly be handled like a painting and enriched with illuminations, something that was profoundly foreign to the papyrus scroll. One cannot see these illuminated manuscripts without being struck by their fusion of letter and image. Reading becomes a polysemiotic experience in which the perception of the image, which is far from a mere illustration, enables readers to recreate in their own mental space the tensions and emotions experienced by the artist. The readable gradually moves into the realm of the visible.[6]

The sight of the codex open on its lectern is emblematic of a religion whose ideal was that all people should be able to read the sacred texts and share the Revelation. Various other innovations gave rise to a change in the reader's relationship to the text and to reading. They include the insertion of spaces between the words in Latin texts, which began about 700 CE in Irish *scriptoria* (*Book of Kells*) and led to decisive changes in the formatting of text.[7] The period from the eleventh to the thirteenth century saw the consolidation of many features that allowed readers to escape the original linearity of speech, such as the table of contents, the index, and the header. Paragraph breaks indicated in the text by a pilcrow (¶) made it easier for readers to deal with units of meaning and helped them to follow the main divisions in the text.

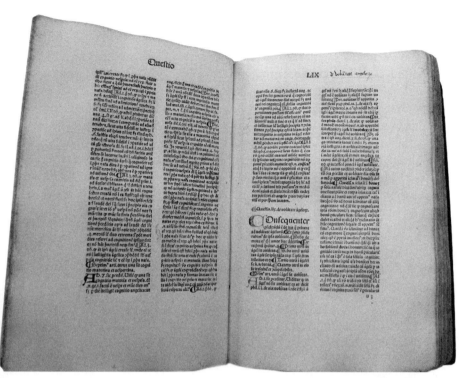

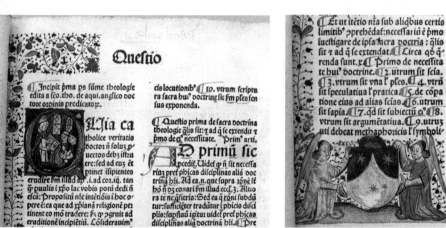

This *incunabulum* from Thomas Aquinas's *Summa Theologica*, printed in 1477 in Venice, follows the manuscript tradition. The decorated initials and paragraph marks are hand-drawn. The first lines are in larger letters. There is no pagination. The layout of the text in two columns and its organization in the form of questions and answers, however, make it very readable. The illuminations are intensely symbolic. The first page (bottom left) is illustrated with an image that depicts the teaching of Thomas Aquinas. At the base of the column, an image depicts the reception of the work by angels (bottom right). (Source: Queen's University.)

In the fifteenth century, the printing revolution was another time of intense reflection on the organization of the book. Febvre and Martin[8] note that the title page made its appearance—finally!—around 1480. After the infancy of the modern book, the period of *incunabula*—books that imitated manuscripts as faithfully as possible—printers quickly saw the full potential of the page as a discrete semiotic space.

Page numbering, which became common in the mid-sixteenth century, enabled readers to better control the duration and pace of their reading and facilitated the discussion of texts by making it possible for readers of the same

This book of hours published by Thielman Kerver in Paris in 1511 is a cross between an almanac and a prayer book and is still very much in the manuscript tradition, but without its richness and beauty. The page is a space not only to be read, but to be explored visually in its various dimensions. It is lavishly illustrated; the text is framed with borders and contains many decorated initials. Key words are in red ink. The book is not paginated but it contains a table of contents. (Source: *Horae divinae virginis Mariae secum verum usum Romanum cum aliis multis folio sequenti notatis*, Queen's University.)

edition to refer to the same passage. Once this step was taken, the move-ment toward tabularization intensified, and sophisticated techniques allowing multiple points of entry into the text became widely used, such as paragraph summaries in the margin and the running head. It was now possible for readers to precisely locate the point they had reached in their reading and to compare the relative size of different sections—in short, to control their read-ing progress. They could also forget the details of what they had read earlier, since they could quickly find them again by referring to a table of contents or index. They could read only the parts of a book that interested them.

Especially if a book is long, readers often construct the meaning on the basis of clues of various types. Typographical markers such as bold, capitals, italics, or color allow them to quickly classify the elements they read and to avoid ambiguity; for example, the italicization of foreign words prevents con-

In this edition of Virgil printed in Basel in 1544, glosses by Servius and Donat surround the text as in a manuscript. The commentary is continuous so as not to waste space, but the numbering of the lines provides tabular information that is useful for shared reading. (Source: University of Ottawa.)

fusion with homonyms. When justified by the material, an index of proper names, a detailed index, or a bibliography permits readers to choose the way of accessing the text that best suits their information needs of the moment. These reading aids did not come into use all at once but were slowly refined, in a process that culminated in the golden age of print in the nineteenth century, when the progress of mechanization heralded the triumph of the printed page. The table of contents, for example, appeared in the twelfth century. The paragraph break, the concept of which had been expressed through the use of the pilcrow in manuscripts of the eleventh century, was finally indicated by a line break, as seen in an edition of *Gargantua* printed in Lyon in 1537. Thus shaped by the ergonomics of the codex, the text was no longer a linear *thread* that was unreeled, but a *surface* whose content could be perceived from various perspectives. These reading aids, which allow readers to consider the text the same way they look at a painting or tableau, are here called tabular.

With the introduction of printing, the art of publishing fluctuated between the temptations of textual continuity and those of pictorial page layout. On the one hand, an austere layout in which the text was rigidly aligned within the frame of the page was best for emphasizing the mechanical perfection of printing and the linear aspect of language and reading; on the other hand, publishers could also be tempted by a complex layout in which the text was presented in different visual blocks among which readers could pick and choose as they wished, exploring their relationships in nonsequential order. These fluctuations in the ideal of the book can be observed across different periods. In this regard, it is informative to compare some of the printing manuals studied by the typography expert Fernand Baudin. A manual published by the printer Fertel in 1723, entitled *La science pratique de l'imprimerie*, is a model of complex layout in which marginal glosses sometimes spill over into the space of the main text. In contrast, a manual published forty years later, written by Fournier, presents the text in a single, rather narrow column and seems to have gone back to the linear order. As for the book by Baudin, who was himself a typographer and wished to give an account of an art that was the passion of his life, it is in large format, with a column of glosses and cross-references systematically running down one side of the main column and sometimes even framing it, as Fertel's glosses do.

The challenge of printed text, in short, is to strike a balance between semantic and visual demands, the ideal obviously being a combination of these two modes of access to the text around a coherent focus. We can still observe the naïve triumph of the visual over the semantic in even the titles of

A collection of Savonarola's sermons published in 1543. The layout of the title is governed by purely visual considerations, which is typical of books printed in this period. The arbitrary word breaks suggest an oral form of reading that was not far in the past. (Source: *Prediche nuovamente venute in luce del reverendo Padre Fra Girolamo Savonarola da Ferrara*, Queen's University.)

sixteenth-century books, in which printers did not hesitate to cut out words in order to create a symmetrical effect.

For Walter Ong, this segmentation shows that reading did not focus on the visual aspect of the words grasped globally, but was still based on oral practices; the presentation of the text was independent of its semantic aspect. It is also likely that such practices involved a kind of playful allusion to a way of reading that was already seen as outmoded.

Today, publishers make such effort to enable the reader to perceive complete words that they sometimes hesitate to break a word at the end of a line, and thus to use justified text, although that was the typographical ideal for centuries, beginning in the time of the *volumen*. This concern with matching the semantic unit with the unit of visual perception is also evident in

Bernal Diaz del Castillo, *Historia verdadera de la conquista de la Nueva España*, Madrid 1632. The text is arranged in two rather narrow columns. The detailed chapter titles and the summaries in the margins enable readers to go directly to passages that interest them. Because of the division into columns, the basic unit is the double page, with one page number and a header extending across the two pages.

magazines, which tend increasingly to make the text of articles fit into the space of the page or double page.

It is now commonly acknowledged that the revolution of the codex was not limited to ergonomics, but that it also had an impact on the nature of content and the evolution of mentalities in general. Indeed, once a text is perceived as a visual entity, and no longer as primarily oral, it lends itself much more readily to criticism. The eye, given the richness of optic nerve endings in the cortex, can mobilize the analytical faculties more easily and more precisely than the ear. As historian Henri-Jean Martin notes on the revolution of printing in the sixteenth century: "By the same token, any reasoned argument was as if detached from the realms of God and men and took on an objective existence. The written text became amoral because it detached from the writing process and no longer demanded that the reader take on responsibility for it by reading it aloud. This may have facilitated heretical propositions."[9]

The process by which the text became an autonomous object crossed a new threshold during the Enlightenment, when the last barriers to its generalized objectification collapsed. That era coincided precisely with spectacular growth in reading in Europe. We will come back to this question.

With the advent of newspapers and the mass-circulation press, which underwent rapid expansion in the nineteenth century, the formatting of text became even more tabular. In a radical departure from the original linearity of speech, text was now presented in the form of visual blocks that complemented and responded to each other on the eye-catching surface of the page. McLuhan gave a name to the metaphor implicit in this arrangement: the "mosaic" text. Indeed, newspapers provide a textual mosaic, in which the reading of various types of information is subtly influenced by the surrounding news, as has been pointed out by analysts of newspaper layout: "For about a century, newspapers have been laid out in such a way that each item of information, though flat on the page, stands out by virtue of the mere fact of its coexistence with other items of information on the page, which in turn acquire their value from this competition."[10] The same authors note that until the end of the nineteenth century, newspapers consisted simply of vertically aligned columns, each of which theoretically constituted a page that went on without interruption. "This type of layout naturally favored a temporal sequence of discourse: there were no interruptions for turning pages, no illustrations to create a break or suspension of reading, and no lead or subheading introducing secondary material. This form corresponds exactly to the temporal logic of discourse: It is the presentation of logos in movement, and not the staging of an event."[11]

The sudden appearance of banner headlines was the beginning of a new kind of layout, one no longer guided by the logic of discourse, but by a spatial logic. "The number of columns, the use of rules, the weight of the type, the font, the position of illustrations, and the use of color make it possible to bring together or move apart, to select, and to separate the units that, in the newspaper, are units of information. Layout then emerges as a rhetoric of space that destructures the order of discourse (its temporal logic) to reconstitute an original discourse, which is precisely the discourse of the newspaper."[12]

Today, there is no doubt that tabularity meets the formatting requirements of information texts in that it allows the reader to apprehend them most effectively. This is especially apparent in magazines, where the dominant model involves framing textual material by means of a hierarchy of titles: section heading, main heading and subheadings. A more substantial article will often be presented in the form of a feature story that, in addition to the main text, includes one or more sidebars elaborating on points raised in the main text. Such fragmented layouts are sometimes criticized. Their primary function is clearly to hold on to readers whose attention span is unsteady or short, unlike a linear format, which is intended for the "serious reader." This way of breaking up text into different elements is also very well suited for communicating a variety of information that readers can select according to their interests. On the other hand, popular magazines may diverge a bit from this ideal and give predominance to glossy ads and photographs in order to entice the reader to leaf through their pages and absorb the discourse of advertising.

When tabularity is taken into account, then, printed text is not exclusively linear and tends to incorporate characteristics of the visual realm. Readers are thus able to free themselves from the thread of the text and go directly to relevant elements. A book may thus be said to be *tabular* when it involves the simultaneous spatial presentation and highlighting of various elements that may help readers identify the connections and find information that interests them as quickly as possible.

The concept of tabularity thus covers at least two distinct phenomena—in addition to designating an internal arrangement of data. On the one hand, it refers to the various organizational means that facilitate access to the content of the text: This is *functional tabularity*, as shown in tables of contents, indexes, and division into chapters and paragraphs. On the other hand, tabularity also suggests that the page may be viewed in the same way as a painting and may include data from various hierarchical levels: This is *visual tabularity*, which enables readers to switch from reading the main text to reading notes, glosses, figures, or illustrations, all of which are present within the space of the double page. This visual tabularity, which is seen primarily in newspapers and magazines, is also found in varying degrees in scholarly books, which may present various types of text juxtaposed on a single page. It is obviously highly developed in electronic publishing, as seen on the Web pages of major newspapers, magazines, and encyclopedias. In addition, through a hybridization of publishing techniques, the layout of books or magazines increasingly borrows from the methods of electronic publishing, such as the use of color, underlining, and marking of text elements, with cross-references to thumbnails or sidebars. In this type of tabularity, the text is shaped like visual material, with blocks referring to each other on the page surface and sometimes incorporating illustrations.

The spatial projection of the thread of the text obviously depends on the format of the book. The smaller the book, the less manipulation of the visual blocks is possible; readers are confined to a continuous movement through a single column of text with no interruption. This format, which was adopted, for example, by the famous French collection Bibliothèque de la Pléiade, tends to reinforce the ideal of a linear typography with nothing to break its regularity. It is especially well suited to novels, which are read for content. National traditions prevent French publishers from placing the table of contents at the front of the book as it is in the English-speaking world, a position better suited to the tabular ideal and to readers' needs.

It should be added, however, that the degree of tabularity of a book will also depend on its content and intended use. Thus, children's books often do not have page numbers: young readers have no need for them, since these books are designed to be read or looked at from cover to cover and there is no expectation of a reflective reading with note taking or references. Scholarly books, which are intended for readers for whom time is valuable, have many tabular guideposts: volumes, chapters, sections, paragraphs, headers, notes, introductory summaries, detailed index, index of proper names, and bibliography. But the linear thread may still be a justifiable choice for developing an argument, insofar as the author wishes to ensure that the reader follows the entire proof. On the other hand, the novel, which is derived from the ancient art of the storyteller, generally demands sustained reading and does not require elaborate tabular clues. The large number of chapters and the hierarchy of sections in Victor Hugo's novels, which often have a very linear narrative thread, may be explained by the fact that these novels were initially published in serial form in newspapers. Today, some writers, anxious to make their readers read continuously and to have their work seen as high literature, as different as possible from the tabular format of the magazine, dispense altogether with chapters, and even paragraphs and punctuation.

9

Meaning and Effect

What is meaning? If we examine this term in reference only to the field of language, we observe that meaning is commonly seen as a given, something that preexists our perception of it. We seek "the meaning of a text," and we say, for example, that a sentence "has a deeper meaning than we would have thought." Usually implicit, the necessary backdrop to any discursive activity, meaning is the horizon against which our judgments are erected. Its importance is most often perceived when it is absent. It is then that we hear the spontaneous comment "that doesn't mean anything" from someone who reads a text without understanding it, or its corollary, "there, that means something," when the reader, through an operation on the materiality of the text or the use of his or her own interpretive filters, succeeds in restoring the conditions for the viability of meaning. We are so accustomed to setting up our own context of understanding as a universal referent that we end up believing that meaning is an objective value, the reality of which is mysteriously incorporated into texts. Even semioticians such as Greimas and Courtés succumb to this tendency when they maintain that "comprehension may be identified with the definition of the concept, itself assimilated to name."[1] This reduction of a mental process to simple lexical content is clearly an extreme form of what can only be called a fear of psychologism.

As Mikhail Bakhtin points out, however, "meaning cannot be dissolved into concept."[2] Indeed, meaning has no existence except in the mind that comprehends. In the final analysis, it corresponds to the pseudo-objective projection of the faith people have in their capacity to understand. Far from being a given, meaning is the product of our activity of comprehension or expression and exists only in the process through which it is born. As Jean-Paul Sartre said in one of his illuminating texts on reading, "meaning is not the sum of words, it is their organic totality."[3] We must therefore look at the question of meaning for the reader in terms of the cognitive activity that creates this meaning, that is, comprehension, an operation that is inherent in the human condition and is part of our everyday experience from a very early age. An act of understanding is accompanied by a particular feeling of completion, comparable to the effect produced by the discovery of the "right form" in Gestalt theory. This sensation is the manifestation of meaning, while signification is only the paraphrase one can give of one's comprehension.

But what is comprehension? According to the etymology of the word, which comes from Latin, comprehension consists in "taking together." At the heart of the concept of comprehension lies the idea that there must be at least two pieces of information or two sets of information for the act of comprehension to occur. This conception has been validated by many studies in cognitive psychology. For J. D. Bransford and K. E. Nitsch, comprehension consists in a successful pairing involving not two pieces of information on the same level, but a cognitive-perceptual situation or context and a piece of information, with the situational context being the primary focus of comprehension activities: "Understanding involves grasping the significance of an input for the situation at hand."[4] This theory of comprehension provides the basis for my discussion here.

An element perceived by our senses and offered for comprehension can be understood only insofar as it is interpreted through what I will call the cognitive context, which consists of information stored in short-term or long-term memory, such as experiences, concepts, or quite broad structures ranging from simple propositions to the summary of a text or even a whole novel one has just read. The cognitive context has been thoroughly studied since the last quarter of the twentieth century and has been given various designations: schema, script, scenario, frame of reference, and so on.[5] Although these terms are not exactly equivalent, they all refer to a complex reality whose operation can only be reconstructed hypothetically. After an initial period in the seventies, when the schema tended to be seen as a stable given, a much more nuanced concept became accepted, that of an extremely fluid entity that can be recomposed from various elements to suit the needs of the situation. One of the most elaborate models is that of Marvin Minsky, in which a multitude of specialized "agents" organized in hierarchies of degree of complexity enable a person to perceive, reason, act, or remember.[6] These agents constitute the cognitive context by means of which a subject is able to produce meaning from data he or she processes. Since this context is the instrument of comprehension, it is especially difficult to identify—just as the eye cannot perceive its own existence in the absence of a mirror or the gaze of another.

The case of misunderstanding is a good example of the failure of the operation of comprehension, because it brings out the disparity that may exist between external information and the cognitive context on the basis of which an initial interpretation was made. According to Henri Bergson's theory as revised by Paul Valéry, laughter is a salutary reaction to the failure of our automatic responses to correctly comprehend, and its purpose is to relieve the mental tension resulting from the awareness of a mistake.[7] Another way to observe the role of cognitive context is to compare a conversation between people who are old friends with one between people who are not. While the former will often understand each other implicitly without many words, the latter will need to spell everything out in order to be able to communicate effectively.

The functioning of a sentence provides a "scale model" of the operation of comprehension. In a minimal sentence, it is usually possible to see an interplay between two elements, one that serves as the initial context and another that modalizes that context. In a dialogue, the context is constantly open to negotiation between interlocutors. A question serves as a context to which a piece of information will be added as a reply, becoming in turn the context for the next question. At its simplest level, then, language functions by providing a context in the position of subject, which is then modalized by a verb and possibly an attribute or a complement, to produce sentences: "The cat is on the mat," "The table is green," and so on. In textual grammar, we say that in these sentences, the subject is the theme (the cat / the table) while what is said about it is the rheme, or predicate ("is on the mat" / "is green"). A sentence may also contain an accumulation of microcontexts: "They returned therefore in good spirits to Longbourn, the village where they lived, and of which they were the principal inhabitants."[8]

In oral language, because the syntactic division is indicated by the prosodic elements, the various components of the sentence can simply be strung together, as for example in "My sister, her favorite fruit is pineapples," or "With cats, what they really like is sleeping." In the latter sentence, the first element suggests a frame of reference related to cats, while the second one refers to another frame of reference, that of their favorite activity, and the final element provides information that connects the contexts previously opened up, while specifying the scope. Oral syntax tends to organize the contexts the listener will need to open up in a sequence going from known to unknown, and to give new information only at the end, where it can much more readily be decoded because it is more expected and better contextualized. Comprehension comes when the various elements finally fit together to form a cognitive whole, with the complete sentence determining the specific meaning of each of the words. As the examples given here show, there is no difference in nature between context and information; any information can serve as the context for the interpretation of new information. Its status as information or context depends on its position in the utterance.

In written language, the situation is a bit more complex. It was long believed in linguistics that it was possible to interpret utterances by hypothesizing a "null context," as if the words of a language could convey a meaning that was fixed and complete in itself. John Searle showed that such a conception was untenable, particularly for isolated utterances. This being said, the context can to a certain extent be constrained by the text. Since the primary function of text is to make it possible to dispense with the presence of the person making the utterance, it should ideally aim to create a reception context that is equivalent for all readers and therefore should foresee the various elements they will need in order to prevent any deviations or misinterpretations. This movement toward a greater autonomy of text with regard to speech was reinforced with the advent of print.[9]

The essential characteristic of written language that profoundly distinguishes it from images is the fact that it functions in a coded, regular way, in both the production and comprehension of significations. In a text, signs are organized in a linear fashion in syntactic configurations that the reader has learned to identify and process. Thanks to this order of signs, an individual can become literate, that is, he or she can, through a long learning process, develop cognitive routines capable of automatically carrying out most of the operations involved in decoding written language, processing it quickly and effectively. In the operation of reading, the fusion of a piece of information with a context has the effect, as in oral language, of creating a new context with which the next piece of information will be placed in relation. The reader may therefore be required only to establish the initial context; other contexts will normally be constructed through the text by means of the cognitive processing of the information being read. As long as readers can relate new information to a previous context, they are moving through familiar territory, guided by their own reading activity. They act like a loom's shuttle, repeatedly incorporating threads taken from the surface of the text into the mental fabric woven on the warp of text already read or retrieved from previous knowledge. This fabric acts as the context or matrix against which a new element will have meaning; reading thus becomes a constant movement, a machine fueled by its own constantly renewed momentum. And this machine for weaving meaning is extraordinarily efficient, as shown by the fact that, while people can speak some hundred words a minute, they are able to read two to ten times as many. Hence, perhaps, our civilization's fascination with the machine, and the affinity of text with the processes of mechanization, as is shown most clearly in the principles of typographic uniformity. According to Paul Valéry, that astute observer of the human mind, "Every man tends to become a machine. Habit, method, mastery, finally—that means machine."[10] Further on, he notes the negative aspects of this: "Automatic responses tend to increase. The possible connections made tend to be modeled on the reflex. Uniformity tends to dominate."[11]

Common experience confirms the close relationship between "automatization" and uniformity. As we have seen, uniformity in reading is brought about through standards of readability that operate at every level of the text. Through the operation of reading, a context is selected from the subject's cognitive networks and placed in relation with the data provided by the text being read, producing effects of comprehension that will be repeated in a continuous, and in principle flawless, chain. Marcel Proust, who was acutely aware of this mechanical aspect of reading, compared his experience in reading Gustave Flaubert's novels to that of being on a moving platform: "And it is not possible for anyone who has one day stepped onto that great Moving Platform of Flaubert's pages, rolling by in a continuous procession, monotonously, dully, indefinitely, to be unaware that they are without precedent in literature."[12] But Flaubert is far from alone in this, since the basic strategy of traditional writing, at least from the perspective of readability, is to ensure that the contexts and data are continuously connected, with as few discontinuities as possible. This movement is brought to perfection in prose that aims to inform. But if narrative suspense is added to prose, its effectiveness is increased and we get the realistic novel, which reached full maturity in the first half of the nineteenth century.

This mechanization is of course theoretical, since the reader's mind may at any time tire and begin to wander from the text, either because mental configurations that compete with those motivating reading suddenly become dominant or because the text evokes strong associations that induce the reader to follow his or her own thoughts. In order to prevent this, some texts tend to saturate the contexts, as if to plug all the interstices through which the subjectivity of the reader could be reintroduced, if such an undertaking were possible. The imaginary space delimited by the text may then be so univocal that it becomes smothering, as in certain of Émile Zola's novels, in which the reader may feel caught up in some diabolical machine leading to an all-too-predictable and inevitable end. In contrast, other texts will accumulate what Wolfgang Iser[13] calls "gaps," "blanks," or "elements of indeterminacy." For Iser, the gaps in the text are a way through which literary writing elicits maximum investment from the reader. The first theorists of literary hypertext took up these concepts, without realizing that these gaps may become chasms into which the reader stumbles and then loses any desire to fill, for lack of a rewarding pact of reading. We will come back to this.

It should be noted that the readability of a text is no guarantee that it will be interesting, since we can mechanically read a story and forget it as soon as we close the book. There will always be a tension between readability requirements, which are needed to enable readers to move with ease through a text to find what interests them, and the personal and original ways writers employ language, using the devices offered by rhetoric. Since its codification in ancient Greece, rhetoric has strived precisely to identify what is irreducible in language and gives it its particular strength, exploring its possibilities for introducing elements of ambiguity or novelty that will have an impact on readers and leave a lasting impression on their memory. This possibility of play on the margins of natural language pushes back the theoretical horizon of an absolute mechanization of meaning, and it is what distinguishes rhetoric from mathematical language. Mathematical language, as we know, can always be paraphrased, in the sense that one equation can be replaced by another without loss of meaning: 4 is equivalent to $2 + 2$ or $3 + 1$ or $1 + 3$ or $5 - 1$, and so on. In contrast, a verbal utterance has no exact equivalent, and synonyms are never more than partial and approximate. The meaning potentially produced always exceeds the strict needs of communication. Generally, this does not prevent language from producing chains of signification that are precise enough to enable social communication. But it is through the always available surplus of meaning that the rhetorical gap can be created, and this is where individuals find a space for play, imagination, and freedom.

In order to better account for this rhetorical dimension and other related aspects of language, it is necessary here to make a distinction between meaning and effect, two facets of cognitive functioning that, to me, correspond roughly to the split between analytical reason and holistic perception. Meaning, as we have seen, originates in the successful synthesis of a context and a piece of information. Being the result of comprehension, it is experienced by the subject as an act carried out at the highest level of consciousness. Linguistically, the verbs referring to this act clearly express the eminently active dimension of comprehension, which is always transitive: The subject *makes* sense, understands or interprets *something*, and so on. The characteristic structure of language is ideally suited for producing meaning.

While meaning is a product of the cognitive system, effect is experienced as a change of state undergone by a subject. *Meaning* is active, while *effect* is passive. In everyday language, subjects say they *experience* an effect or that something *has an effect* on them, as if their cognitive system were the arena of events external to them, events that are perceived holistically rather than being analyzed, felt rather than thought. Music is naturally suited for creating effects, as is painting; this is even more the case for the world of tastes and smells, which are often perceived subliminally but are nonetheless very effective in reviving traces of memory or triggering emotional reactions, as in the famous episode of the *madeleine* dipped in tea narrated by Marcel Proust.

The language of poetry differs profoundly from scientific language in that effects play an essential role in it. Some poets have stated explicitly that their work belongs to the realm of effect rather than that of meaning. Thus Robert Desnos, in answer to a question about his poetry, exclaimed: "Explain what? There is nothing to explain in poetry, only to experience. Poetry is unique, whole, and open to all. It is up to you to experience it."[14]

It should be stressed that meaning and effect are not mutually exclusive, since perception of an effect may occur in parallel with the processing of a meaning. It is possible to read while listening to music, or to talk with a person while being aware of the olfactory and visual signals he or she is emitting, and these common experiences confirm the validity of the distinction made in everyday language between meaning and effect. These two mental realities are different in nature and therefore draw upon different cognitive resources. Were this not the case, they could not be perceived in the same act of comprehension. We know, for example, that a subject cannot simultaneously perceive two different figures in one image, whether it be an ambiguous painting by M. C. Escher or one of the classic experiments on the perception of optical illusions, such as the one representing either an hourglass or two silhouettes facing each other, the one of either a young woman in a fur hat or an old witch, or the Necker Cube.[15] Marvin Minsky analyses these observations on perception as indicative of the way our minds function: "The drawing on the right looks like a cube—but first it looks like a cube as seen from above and then, suddenly, it looks like a cube as seen from below. Why does each drawing seem to change its character from time to time? Why can't we see both forms at once? Because, it seems, our agencies can tolerate just one interpretation at a time."[16] Or, to put it in other words, "We cannot perform two different operations simultaneously with the same message."[17]

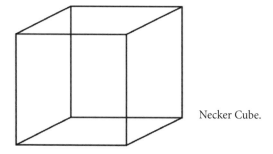

Necker Cube.

Drawing all the consequences of these observations, I will posit that if we can read a poem while experiencing its effects of rhythm and sound, this clearly indicates that the production of meaning does not mobilize the same cognitive resources as the perception of the effects of language. Since the brain involves many specialized agencies, it is legitimate to hypothesize that meaning is produced through the central agency of attention, while effects are processed locally through sensory perception. The musicality of verse would thus mobilize the agencies directly related to the auditory canal, while the richness of an illumination in a manuscript would draw on those that are specialized in visual processing. The central agency, which is also the site of attention, handles specifically semantic operations. These different agencies are not absolutely hermetic, and local saturation will lead to a spillover of data into the central agency, which will then take into consideration the signs relayed by the local level. If the effects are too powerful, the mind will simply stop concentrating on meaning.

The critic I. A. Richards, examining the barrier that poetic form puts up against comprehension, compared the difficulty in understanding poetry to the difficulty one may have performing delicate intellectual operations in a noisy environment.[18] Similarly, the verbal dimension of an opera libretto is generally submerged by the sound and visual effects, because while the brain is remarkably capable of carrying out various processes in parallel, the effectiveness of the central processing may be weakened or even blocked by overly invasive effects.

Conversely, the processing of meaning will be facilitated if the effects are kept under control or neutralized. The space of the page, with its margins, color, and typography, produces visual effects that may elicit readers' attention but also distract them from reading. The nature of the semantic operations required of the reader may make it advisable to neutralize visual effects by using regular typography and a simple layout. Consequently, the typographic ideal has long been to be "invisible." If the typographic effects are too intrusive, they hinder reading of the text, and the reader becomes caught up in the contemplation of the formal aspects and neglects the linguistic material. Johanna Drucker states, "The literary text wants no visual interference or manipulation to disturb the linguistic enunciation of the verbal matter. All interference, resistance, must be minimized in order to allow the reader a smooth reading of the unfolding linear sequence. The aspirations of typographers serving the literary muse are to make the text as uniform, as neutral, as accessible and seamless as possible, and it remains the dominant model for works of literature, authoritative scholarly prose, and any other printed form in which seriousness of purpose collapses with the authority of the writer, effacing both behind the implicit truth value of the words themselves."[19]

The signs that produce effects are not necessarily different in nature from those that produce meaning. For example, the application of the color blue to a segment of text may be intended to create a simple visual effect, just as it may be used, according to a convention, to highlight a word or indicate a hypertext link. All signs can therefore be subjected to semiotic analysis, but not all of them are part of the same system of signification or have the same textual function. More generally, the realm of the perceived elicits our understanding when it is presented as a question or an answer to a question.

Unlike visual or prosodic effects, rhetorical effects are produced directly at the level of the processing of language, whether this involves play with the form of words, syntax, meaning, or the logic of the text. Thus they may all the more easily go unnoticed, as is the case for most figures of speech, notably synecdoche and metonymy, which are invisible to the basic user, for whom they are simple language shortcuts. A rhetorical effect is inevitably perceived after the fact, as supplementary to the central processing, and it is measured by the distance from everyday usage or the degree of ambiguity of the discourse. And this awareness, which forces the subject to reevaluate the semantic processing he or she has just carried out according to the effect perceived, interferes with the meaning and, like visual or auditory effects, gives it a particular coloration. A rhetorical effect is thus comparable to the effect produced by an image. As stated by Jean-François Lyotard: "An imaged text is a discourse which is very close to the figure. It will be necessary, then, to analyze the different ways in which such a proximity may be established: the figurative power of a word, of course, but also the rhythmic power of syntax, and at an even deeper level, the matrix of narrative rhythm, what Propp called form."[20] In spite of their deep differences, image and word may extend their domain onto each other's ground. We shall come back to this question in chapter 21, "The Rise of the Visual."

10

Filters in Reading

Just as filters are used in photography and electroacoustics to select only certain wavelengths of light and sound, the human mind has an innate ability
to filter sensory data through an interpretive grid. It is well known that in
the din of a party, people can easily select from the ambient noise only the
voices that interest them. What is commonly referred to as the "plasticity of
the brain" appears to be related to its capacity to use a variety of filters for the
processing of perception or intellection. These filters provide the context for
operations of overall comprehension. Like their optical counterparts, they
can be superimposed; for example, when reading a Japanese novel from the
eleventh century, readers would use the filters both of their literary knowledge
and of their imagined Japan. The filters will be quite different when reading
an advertisement for a theme park.

While most filters are normally flexible and are chosen according to the
information to be processed, a person can also decide to adopt an all-encom-
passing, doctrinaire point of view almost permanently, and apply it systematically to all data received, regardless of the source; this is an ideological filter.
Racists thus express their prejudices in any situation, just as Communists
were daily able to find confirmation of the superiority of their ideology and
the need for revolution. The adoption of an ideological filter has the advantage of constantly reinforcing the certainty that one is right, because, on the
scales on which any act of verbal comprehension is finally weighed, it is the
context that weighs most heavily.

An ideological filter is a set of simple, explicit propositions that a person
adopts deliberately. This makes it a cognitive phenomenon that is very different from prejudices, received ideas, or stereotypes, which are not a mat-

ter of choice, but are imposed without our knowledge by the simple fact of our immersion in a particular social environment. A stereotype may be abandoned when a person suddenly becomes aware of it or, through education, acquires greater understanding. In contrast, people who have chosen to adopt a particular ideology will energetically avoid facing facts that may contradict or destroy their system of values. The concept of ideology thus includes a militant fervor that a stereotype does not possess.

Since reading involves subjecting one's imagination to the influence of someone else's thoughts, it can lead to radical changes in a person's belief system. For Pascal Quignard, "the fears and accusations of traditional theologians [against reading] are not silly or narrow-minded, [but] result from the fact that many people are remarkably sensitive to reading," and he concludes that "people who read take the risk of losing the little control they have over themselves. They completely submit, while reading, to the possibility of loss of identity, the risk of disappearing."[1]

We certainly pay a price for our dependence on ready-made thoughts. Four hundred years ago, Montaigne already observed: "Our minds work only upon trust, when bound and compelled to follow the appetite of another's fancy, enslaved and captivated under the authority of another's instruction; We have been so subjected to the trammel, that we have no free, nor natural pace of our own."[2] With the unlimited possibilities for reproduction brought about by printing, the political and doctrinal stability of European societies was shattered in the space of a few years. It is difficult to overestimate the impact produced by the publication, in the fifty years following the introduction of printing, of nearly twenty million books, or forty thousand different titles, for a population of a hundred million.[3] The Reformation's debt to printing for the dissemination of Martin Luther's theses is widely acknowledged. It is no wonder then that the production of books was soon subjected to strict regulation. In France the Ordonnance de Montpellier, which was proclaimed in 1537, obliged printers to deposit a copy of every new book published; this was the beginning of legal deposit. In 1566 the Édit de Moulins decreed that no one could print a book without previously obtaining a royal privilege. A similar provision came into force in England in 1538.[4] In addition, church authorities established the rule of the imprimatur, which required that all books of a religious nature be approved by the bishop of the diocese before printing. The Index of Forbidden Books, an official list of works a good Catholic should not read, which had already existed in embryonic forms for several centuries, became really powerful after the Council of Trent and the publication of the bull *Ut Pestiferarum*, by Pope Gregory XIII, in 1572.

The papal bull compared the speed with which radically new ideas could spread through a broad public, subverting the established order, to that of the plague, which was very present in people's concerns and fears.

Such restrictions of readers' free choice did not fall into disuse until the second half of the twentieth century, when the rise of democratic aspirations made it impossible for political authorities to continue to justify censorship; the Index was officially abolished under Pope Paul VI in 1966. Western societies implicitly acknowledge that the regulation of ideas cannot be imposed from above and that, with the exception of hate propaganda, all points of view should be allowed free expression—just as products in a market economy circulate without artificial restriction. This liberalism has been accompanied by an expansion of the social sciences, with a larger role being given to interpretation.

Today, an accomplished reader is no longer defined as someone able to grasp "the correct meaning" but could well be someone with the ability to pass any text through a filter consciously chosen according to specific goals. That is the theme of a story by Jorge Luis Borges,[5] who imagined that deliberate, systematic anachronism could be a powerful way of creating new plays on the meaning of familiar texts, allowing one to read *Don Quixote* as if it had been written by an early twentieth century author or *The Imitation of Christ* as if it had been written by Louis-Ferdinand Céline.

11

Textuality

Form and Substance

According to Oswald Ducrot and Tzvetan Todorov, a text is "defined by its autonomy and by its closure."[1] This classic definition has become problematic, however, since the advent of hypertext. Indeed, hypertext as we know it on the Web can be organized in such a way that it has no apparent limits other than those determined by the reader. Thus escaping the control of its author, the text has left the closed, stable world of the book to move into the realm of the ephemeral and the episodic.

In order to clarify the question, we need a definition of textuality that is not based on a specific medium. Text is extremely fluid and cannot be limited to a mere sequence of words. We know, for example, that a manuscript, once published, becomes a new product, and that the publishing machine brings to bear a very costly infrastructure to make the book an attractive object. We can expect this "packaging" of the text also to change the way it is read. Far from being irrelevant, the medium can change the reader's relationship to a text. A newspaper is not read the same way as a book, and it is hard to imagine the contents of today's newspaper being presented in pocketbook format; similarly, the publication of a novel in newspaper format would make reading it less pleasant and thus less desirable. Even more than its print counterpart, digital text can take a variety of forms, although its potential has still not been exploited to the maximum, given the limitations of today's monitors and software.

To better define the text as object, I will draw on the idea that "every text contains a set of instructions for readers, which enable them to orient themselves in the piece of world presented in the book."[2] In my view, the instructions given to the reader go beyond the purely verbal and beyond what is generally considered the text. To designate the text as apprehended in its visual environment, I will use the concept of textuality, defined as a characteristic of a perceptible object that is apprehended spatially and that addresses a reader's comprehension both by systematically relating simple propositions placed contiguously and by making more or less distant, continuous, and regular references to elements previously presented. This semiotic activity is influenced by the arrangement of the text in the space of the page, its typographic attributes, and its iconic environment, as well as, in the case of text on the screen, by the placement of elements in separate windows accessed through hypertext links. Any manipulation of these variables will have repercussions on textuality and will change the way a given text may be read. For example, the textuality of a narrative will be very different depending on whether it is laid out as a news item, as a poem, or as hypertext. Consider the following rewriting of a news item by Jean Cohen:

Yesterday on Highway 7
An automobile
Going a hundred miles an hour crashed
Into a tree
Its four occupants were
Killed.[3]

At first glance, the arrangement in verse, the elimination of punctuation, and the introduction of a capital letter at the beginning of each line impose a "poetic" reading of this news item. The enjambment of complements and important words ("Into a tree," "Killed") introduces "blanks" into the reading and produces meaning effects very different from those produced by the same text in prose. While prose is normally associated with textuality that plays on the contiguity of various elements of the text and the connections among them, poetry favors a visually fragmented textuality in which all the elements are simultaneously present, and which, through its spatial arrangement, highlights paradigmatic relationships.

We could imagine arranging this news item as a hypertext with the information broken down into seven entries placed in a column on the left, with answers that would appear when the reader clicked on them:

Title? An accident
When? yesterday
Where? on Highway 7

What? an automobile
How? going a hundred miles an hour
Action? crashed into a tree
Result? Its four occupants were killed

This is clearly an extreme example, but it is intended to illustrate a type of textual functioning that is theoretically permitted by hypertext. By extracting the paradigmatic data from their textual and syntactic thread, hypertext objectifies the network of characters and events that are normally woven together in the narrative structure and transforms a living configuration into a large number of *bits* of information. In this, hypertext has a certain similarity with the structure of a database.

Computers can obviously also accommodate traditional forms of textuality such as prose and poetry. But the constraints of reading on a screen and the huge mass of information available on the Web favor a situation in which readers choose to click on information they consider interesting. This characteristic places hypertext within a pragmatics of interactivity.

Textuality does not depend only on the spatial arrangement of the segments of a text, but also on their typographical attributes; the fact that a word is in a particular size of type, a particular typeface, or in bold, italics, color, or upper case indicates to readers that it is to be read differently from the neighboring words. These material characteristics of the text as a visual object were crucial for a poet such as Stéphane Mallarmé, who placed a great deal of importance on the arrangement of the poem on the page

Fury said to
a mouse, That
he met
in the
house,
'Let us
both go
to law:
I will
prosecute
you.—
Come, I'll
take no
denial;
We must
have a
trial:
For
really
this
morning
I've
nothing
to do.'
Said the
mouse to
the cur,
'Such a
trial,
dear sir,
With no
jury or
judge,
would be
wasting
our breath.'
'I'll be
judge,
I'll be
jury,'
Said
cunning
old Fury;
'I'll try
the whole
cause,
and
condemn
you
to
death.' "

Calligram of the mouse in Lewis Carroll, *Alice in Wonderland,* Chapter 3, "A Caucus Race and a Long Tale."

and was as sensitive as a typographer to the value of margins and blank space. Most writers, however, consider these concerns frivolous or as encroachments on the territory of the publisher, the ultimate master of the book's form. For a long time, only the calligram, whose textuality comes from the semantic redundancy of the visual and the textual, could legitimately claim a visual component and preserve it intact in the format of the book.

We must also consider the way in which the iconic environment of the text guides the activity of the reader. We probably do not read a novel in the same way in a text-only edition as in an illustrated edition. With the advent of hypertext, the importance of the visual aspect of the text, of its iconic dimension, is expanding, because authors are able to regain control of the tools of publishing, which the invention of printing had taken from them. Thanks to the computer, they can determine the typographic and iconic form of their texts and the precise degree of interactivity they wish to grant the reader.

In a strictly compartmentalized culture, it was easy to exclude the visual dimension from textuality, but it will no longer be possible to do so when the layout, typography, and iconic elements can be designed by authors themselves and are considered an integral part of the work, making it an object to be looked at as much as read, as in the case of Michel Butor's "book objects."

12

Textual Connections

As we saw in the section on context [chapter 8], meaning is based on the discovery of connections between a piece of information and a preexisting cognitive context. In principle, any textual or nontextual element present in the reader's consciousness can serve as the context for the comprehension of a new sentence, provided that it can be linked to it in some way, whether legitimately or as the result of a misunderstanding.

The text produces its meaning and its effects through the connection of blocks of text at various levels. The connections may be extratextual and may relate a text to a nonlinguistic context. This is the case when a text is associated with an iconic element or with factual or pragmatic information. The production of meaning and effects may also come from an intertextual relationship, in which a text is given resonance by textual elements associated with it. This relationship may be based on a weak, even a purely subliminal, connection through which readers sense something vaguely familiar below the surface. But it may also require a close comparative reading, as in the case of pastiche or parody, where the pleasure of the text comes from the discovery of the ways in which the source text has been travestied.

Most often, a text constitutes a universe of meaning in itself and plays on purely textual connections, that is, on relationships between its propositions, sentences, paragraphs, chapters, or parts. The major units of connection—paragraphs and chapters—allow readers to more easily manipulate large amounts of information, because they stand out visually and acquire an autonomous existence.

In principle, the more levels of connection a text has, the greater the potential production of meaning. The traditional superiority of written language over other forms of expression arises from the fact that text was from the outset conceived in terms of reading, that is, it was designed for reception by an addressee. Also, the very nature of its medium grants readers complete mastery over all its components; every element of the text can be isolated, analyzed, and placed in relation to other elements of the same text, which permits a thorough analysis of the intended or possible meanings. Both on the material level and on the level of significations, the book has a layered structure,[1] which gives readers a grasp over the content that film or other forms of spectacle cannot offer.

I will hypothesize that there are two basic types of discursive organization. The first type corresponds to dialogical or semidialogical utterances of the question–answer type, in which the first term is often left implicit, as in informational and polemical texts, but may also be formulated quite explicitly, as in Thomas Aquinas's *Summa Theologica* (e.g., "Whether love is a passion?" "Whether sin has a cause?"). According to Walter Ong, we have here a "quasi-oral format: each section or 'question' begins with a recitation of objections against the position Thomas will take, then Thomas states his position, and finally answers the objections in order."[2] Incidentally, Aquinas wonders "whether Christ should have committed his teaching to writing" and he answers negatively because "men would have had no deeper thought of His doctrine than that which appears on the surface of the writing";[3] the visual mode was thus deemed very inferior to the oral one, a situation that would eventually begin to change in the Renaissance.

The second type of organization is temporal and belongs to the prototypical autonomous utterance, the narrative ("then . . . and then . . ."). These two forms are derived from the state of primary orality. Later we will consider the case of the list, in which the connections are not discursive but are based on an elementary process of placement in a visual sequence.

A text can produce meaning only if it establishes connections that can be perceived by the user. This implies that the author determines beforehand both the sections of the text and the types of connections to be established between them. The same principles apply to hypertext. In encyclopedic databases, the connections are semidialogical; it is assumed that readers are guided by their curiosity about the phenomena behind the words and have within them the questions the database answers, without excluding the possibility that they are also guided by networks of associations. But the same cannot be said for all types of reading. Often readers cannot find in themselves sufficient impetus to chart an autonomous course; they want to be pulled along, carried on what might be called semantic rails. The perfect answer to this popular demand is the novel, which is a very effective textual "machine," particularly if it is long; a novel of a thousand-plus pages produces a very rich context of reception in the reader's mind and makes possible many meaningful connections. Readers of Harlequin romances, on the other hand, enjoy rediscovering a world that is already familiar. Accustomed to a narrative that takes them by the hand in this way, readers are very likely to feel at a loss when faced with a text that offers only associations of a dialogical kind.

13
Instances of Utterance

The term *utterance* designates the particular way an individual appropriates language in a specific concrete situation. Émile Benveniste defines it as the "activation of language through an individual act of use."[1] He distinguishes two main modes of utterance according to the relationship between what is said and the persons to whom it is said: historical narrative and discourse. It is the latter that interests us here. Contrary to what one might think at first glance, Benveniste's concept of discourse encompasses all language situations, oral and written, in which a speaker directly addresses an interlocutor. In written language, this is the case, for example, in "all the genres in which someone addresses himself to someone, proclaims himself a speaker and organizes what he says in the category of person."[2] Discourse therefore includes correspondence, memoir, drama, and didactic writing. Linguistically, it is marked by the use of deictics ("here," "there," "now," "tomorrow," "yesterday," etc.), certain pronouns ("I," "you," rather than the third person), and certain verb tenses in preference to others.

Let us briefly examine how the medium changes the instance of utterance. In a face-to-face conversation, discourse implicitly refers to the person of the speaker and a context; a great deal of information can thus be omitted because it is part of the knowledge shared between the interlocutors. This is the case, at the very least, for the name, status, and role of each interlocutor, as well as the place and time of the exchange.

On the other hand, as soon as the author of the discourse is absent, this information must be made explicit within the text, in varying degrees depending on the medium. In the case of a message carved in stone, the reference of an adverb of place such as "here" is absolute, in the sense that it is provided by the place where the stone stands. This preservation of the physical place of the utterance gives rise to a certain "presence" of the speaker and authorizes a certain interaction with the reader.

This is no longer true for the printed text, in which the references of deictics have become completely relative. In a nonfiction text, in order to know who is speaking, where, and when, the reader generally has to refer to standardized bibliographic information that is part of the paratext: date of original publication, name of author, publisher, and so on. These elements allow the reader to inscribe the text in its original context of production. It is, possible, however, that a sheet of paper may not include the place or the date of printing or the name of the publisher, or even the name of the author. This erasure of any reference to the instance of utterance is characteristic of the dissemination of anonymous discourse and is anathema to authoritarian regimes.

With the Internet, our civilization has entered a new age in which the "technologizing of the word" is pushed to the extreme and references are much more fluid and haphazard than on paper. Losing in stability what it gains in fluidity, text has become a pure, immaterial configuration with no attachment to a place of origin or even to a specific culture, accelerating the obsolescence of the state apparatus. Even the address of the server where a page is hosted is often of no referential value, since aliases are increasingly common. And many sites can be hosted free on foreign servers that survive on advertising income. In addition, since the concept of page is less firmly established in a hypertext document than in a book and is not dependent on a set order as it would be in a book, discourse is stripped of many elements that would otherwise mark it. Since authors of experimental literary hypertexts cannot take for granted that readers will read their "pages" in any particular order, they cannot use the future or the past tense to provide metadiscursive information, and the story is therefore condemned to unfold in a permanent and monotonous present (or past). Nor can the author of an essay in this medium use spatial substitutes for temporal references, such as "we will see below" or "as we have seen in a previous section." In principle, the only reference permitted is to the text in the current page as opposed to other pages, which are neither previous nor subsequent. Hypertext is where we witness the triumph of the ideology of "here and now."

Once relieved of its "atoms" and reduced to the state of "bits" on the Web, to use Nicholas Negroponte's terms, discourse thus loses a good many of its linguistic mechanisms for self-referential anchoring. But it compensates for this loss by the extensive use of links to other pages that may provide supplementary information. The self-reference, which was present in the book and called upon explicitly, is now indicated, but only partially, by means of a simple visual attribute attached to the word that serves as an anchor point for the hypertext link: color, underlining, or a change in the cursor when it moves over that word. A change in color makes it possible in some cases to situate the link in a temporal dimension, the meaning of which depends not on the activity of the writer but on that of the reader, as a link already visited or to be visited. In this aspect, the reader of hypertext has indeed taken over part of the role that was previously the author's; he or she has become the speaker in the reading relationship between the different parts of the text.

This change in the relationship to references certainly enables readers to find needed information much more quickly. By clicking on an author's name, they can go to that author's home page, and with another click, send that author a message. But to work properly, the use of such implicit references also requires the development of new conventions of writing and reading, without which the visual references will simply not be understood or will be considered irrelevant. For example, the deictic "here" encountered on a Web page cannot refer to a geographic location, since the same document may be found on different servers on different continents. This deictic can only be used if it is "co-textualized," that is, if it specifically refers to the immediate context of the text: "Here" means simply "here." In hypertext, references depend on elements that are present on the same visual plane, in the same window, or on the same screen surface. Once it becomes necessary to click on a button or a word to make a new window appear, that window will be seen as foreign to the initial context, or at least as secondary, like notes pushed to the end of a chapter or volume.

The virtualization of the reference context also affects the author of the text on the computer, who is more anonymous, more of a phantom, than any published writer. The use of pseudonyms is the logical culmination of this decontextualization, which provides no way for readers to know if they are dealing with a man or a woman, a child or an adult. A pure textual entity, the Internet user thus possesses much greater freedom than that won by Western writers of past centuries through the use of the abstract entity of the narrator in fiction. Behind the masks we choose for ourselves, all of us can now write our own lives, exploring all the resources of feigned speech. The spread of English as the lingua franca should further accentuate the rupture with the speaker's initial cultural context. The story of Babel will perhaps be read in the future as a myth about the confusion resulting from the multiplicity not of languages, but of discursive masks or roles.

In this regard, let us recall that in 1966 Joseph Weizenbaum created an interactive program called *Eliza,* which was capable of giving the illusion of an intelligent reaction in its answers to messages sent to it, adopting the discursive role of a nondirective Rogerian psychologist. This is the first example of a "chatterbot"; it has been reworked using conversational patterns characteristic of discussion groups so that it can create an illusory presence and be a valid interlocutor for thousands of Internet users. Researchers at MIT drew on this elementary form of interactivity to create *Zork,* the first interactive fiction computer game. Later, intelligent agents were introduced that act according to complex scenarios designed in terms of "scripts, plans, and goals."[3]

14

From Interactivity to the Pseudo-Text

You are about to begin reading Italo Calvino's
new novel, *If on a Winter's Night a Traveler.* Relax.
Concentrate. Dispel every other thought. Let the
world around you fade. Best to close the door . . .

—Italo Calvino, *If on a Winter's Night a Traveler*

The interactivity of hypertext is based on a combination of factors, two of which seem essential: a dialogic relationship with the reader and the possibility of varied bifurcations of the textual thread. Interactivity, thus, despite its technological appearance, seems to revive certain aspects of orality. But it can go far beyond orality.

Dialogue may be initiated by directly addressing someone. In written language, addressing the reader is often associated with the archaic medium of stone, as if its permanence in a given place gives the utterance its intrinsic force. For example, many epigraphs from ancient Greece have been found that address passers-by, sometimes insulting them, sometimes inviting them to meditate. There are also explicit warnings on the walls of medieval cathedrals, such as the one in Tournai (Belgium), where a Latin inscription sharply admonishes the beer drinker who might be tempted to relieve himself against the building. Tombstones and graffiti also attest to the permanence of writing directly addressing to the reader. But there is a danger that such rough direct speech be perceived as a brutal intrusion into private space, especially in contemporary society.

The dialogic structure is more widespread in works from cultures that are close to a state of orality. It is characteristic, for example, of the early philosophical works of Greek civilization, such as Plato's dialogues. According to Mikhail Bakhtin, this structure can still be found in polemical and informational writing. A close analysis of such texts reveals that, in many cases, the authors anticipate readers' possible objections. This is often apparent in the way the paragraphs are divided, with each one corresponding to a different objection. It is thus possible to see in writing a form of interactivity anticipated by the author, who constructs the text in view of the encounter with the reader.

If we examine things from the reader's point of view, we also see that the work of comprehension is carried out by allowing the thought of an author to be received and then to be processed, evaluated, and accepted as more or less valid; in short, the text will stimulate a response. This analysis of comprehension in terms of dialogue is the basis of the hermeneutics of Hans-Georg Gadamer, for whom any text implies a dialogic relationship with the potential reader: "I believe I have shown clearly that we need to think of oral comprehension in terms of a situation of dialogue, that is, ultimately, in terms of a question-answer dialectic in which the participants explain themselves and articulate a shared world. . . The fact that something is written in no way changes the problematic. . . Moreover, any book that is waiting for the reader's response opens such a dialogue."[1] This concept of dialogue is more abstract than that of Bakhtin, and the "dialogue" referred to by Gadamer may take place entirely in the minds of the readers, who will question the text on the basis of their beliefs and previous knowledge. We are therefore quite far from the dialogic situation of oral language.

The eighteenth century, under the impetus of printing, witnessed the stripping of the author's subjectivity from the text and the culmination of the reification of the word; at the same time, there was an attempt in literature not only to introduce the figure of the reader into the narrative, but to make the reader an important part of the narrative play. The most striking successes in this regard were provided by Laurence Sterne and the French philosopher Denis Diderot, who pushed the practice to the limit, with hilarious results. For example, in *The Life and Opinions of Tristram Shandy, Gentleman*, the narrator does not hesitate to speak directly to the reader: "In the beginning of the last chapter, I inform'd you exactly when I was born; — but I did not inform you, how. No; that particular was reserved entirely for a chapter by itself; — besides, Sir, as you and I are in a manner perfect strangers to each other, it would not have been proper to have let you into too many circumstances relating to myself all at once. — You must have a little patience."[2] In *Jacques the Fatalist and His Master* (*Jacques le Fataliste*), Diderot does something similar, setting himself up as master of the discourse and playing his readers like a virtuoso, as a storyteller might. He imagines questions, which he immediately rejects as irrelevant ("What was their name?—What does it matter to you?"), and waxes ironic with readers, attacking them for asking questions they just might be asking themselves: "Now they're on their horse again and on their way. Where were they on their way to? That's the second time you've asked me that question, and here's the second time I answer: What's it to you?"[3]

But this offhand, humorous way of addressing the reader soon gave way to more discreet approaches marked by the use of the third person, as in the great novels of the nineteenth century. "In winding up Mistress Fanshawe's memoirs, the reader will no doubt expect to hear that she came finally to bitter expiation of her youthful levities. Of course, a large share of suffering lies in reserve for her future."[4] "To be a saloon-keeper and kill a man was to be illustrious. Hence the reader will not be surprised to learn that more than one man was killed in Nevada under hardly the pretext of provocation."[5]

Today, even such respectful allusions to the reader are rare. The possibility still exists—and Italo Calvino, for example, has used it with great success in his famous novel *If on a Winter's Night a Traveler*. But the role of the narratee generally survives in writing merely as a ghostly trace that only a patient and attentive reader can reconstruct. In Gerald Prince's model, this is done by examining the rhetorical questions, overjustifications, and comparisons related to a referent supposedly familiar to the intended readership.

Contemporary readers project themselves most readily into the position of observers rather than direct interlocutors; they would rather read over the writer's shoulder than be considered the writer's toy or be treated as captive addressees in a face-to-face dialogue. In short, they are not prepared to give up the comfortable position they have enjoyed since reading went from the domain of the voice, a projection of the body articulating it, to that of the gaze, with all the distancing that position allows. No one is more aware of this change than writers, since a writer is first and foremost an accomplished reader. The unequal relationship between author and reader therefore tends to be concealed, even denied, in contemporary literature, rather than dramatically foregrounded as it is in Diderot and Sterne. While young readers may of necessity still quite readily accept an unequal relationship, the same cannot be said of sophisticated adult readers. They do not have much tolerance for writers who abuse their power and they are not prepared to place them in a position of enunciative superiority—just as they reject narrative inconsistencies and implausibilities when they feel their capacity to anticipate and reason is being underestimated. If it can still be said that writing is the site of a dialogue between narrator and reader, this is most often in a veiled form that takes place within the act of comprehension.

This kind of dialogical interaction is thus one of the primary components of interactivity, which harks back to the ancient capacity of writing to directly address the reader; it is something the modern text has learned to do with extreme discretion. But dialogue alone is not sufficient to create interactivity; it must be integrated into a text or hypermedia that is subject to significant modification in accordance with the reader's responses.

Anticipating the concept of hypertext and the virtual labyrinth, Borges provided various fascinating allegories of the infinite book. One of them is "The Garden of Forking Paths," first published in Spanish in 1941, in which he imagines that a Chinese professor has spent many years writing a strange and seemingly incoherent novel that is like a "labyrinth of symbols" or "an invisible labyrinth of time." The key to this enigma is provided when an English scholar explains that the incoherence of the novel arises from the fact that the author has included all the possible outcomes for every event in the narrative. The contradictions and incompatibilities of the novel are thus due to the juxtaposition of all these possibilities within a single narrative framework. Once the enigma has been explained, the narrative can conclude with an ending whose impact is all the more powerful for being rigorously logical and providing an ironic counterpoint to the hypothesis of infinite possibilities that is the central theme of the story. It should be noted that the paradox here does not lie in the idea that the Chinese professor's novel describes an infinite movement through *many* texts—since a library already offers this experience without it being seen as anything out of the ordinary. The powerful paradox of the story lies in its imagining such movement within a single book, a book whose organizing principle is this very idea. In short, this story by Borges establishes the concept of the branching narrative. What remained was for it to be implemented effectively.

One of the first such achievements was "Un conte à votre façon" ["A story as you like it"], published in 1967 by Raymond Queneau, whose interest in combinatorial literature had already given rise to the famous *Cent mille milliards de poèmes* (translated as *One Hundred Million Million Poems)* and was reflected in his important contribution to Oulipo (Ouvroir de Littérature Potentielle [Workshop of Potential Literature]). The story consists of twenty paragraphs, constructed on the model of a children's tale—a form ideally suited to intense interaction with the reader:

1. Do you wish to hear the story of the three alert peas?
   - if yes, go to 4
   - if no, go to 2
2. Would you prefer the story of the three big skinny beanpoles?[6]

It should be noted that at the time when Queneau was writing this story, narratology was undergoing extraordinary expansion. In the wake of Claude Lévi-Strauss's studies of myth and Vladimir Propp's work on the folktale, theorists such as Roland Barthes, A. J. Greimas, Paul Larivaille, and Henri Bremond were producing studies of the logic of narrative possibilities. This new look at the structure of narrative enabled it to be reinvented in an interactive form.

A further step in this area came from studies of gaming, which showed the superiority of random combinations, such as those produced by throwing dice. In England, Steve Jackson and Ian Livingstone, who were fans of role-playing games such as *Dungeons and Dragons*, took a active interest in the branching structure and developed a narrative genre that quickly became very popular among young people under the title *Fighting Fantasy Gamebooks*. In this type of book, each paragraph is numbered and leads to a variety of choices, some of which may force the reader to backtrack or to end the narrative prematurely. This type of narrative structure requires that at the outset the author establish an organizational chart precisely detailing the branchings, so as not to get lost or lose the reader, since the number of paragraphs is far greater than in Queneau's story—400 paragraphs for *The Warlock of Firetop Mountain*, the first volume in the series, published in 1982, and 800 for the longest one, *The Crown of Kings* (1985). The formula worked, and it even inspired serious essays.[7] After writing twenty-eight titles on this model, however, Jackson and Livingstone quite logically turned to computer games, which permitted incomparably richer interactivity.

On the computer, however, especially in games, interactivity does not necessarily occur through dialogue. In fact, the verbal component, which was still very present in the games of the eighties, has now become much more limited. Even complex fictions may make minimal use of language other than in the introductory narrative. This "deverbalization" was made possible by a radical change in the narrative point of view. Indeed, the "readers" of these interactive fictions are often not in the position of being told a story that already exists or witnessing it taking place in front of them, as is the case in a novel or a film. Nor are they participants in a dialogue they do not control, or limited to making choices among possibilities offered by the author. With first-person games, the player is really the hero, the protagonist through whom the story comes to life and moves forward. The player's introduction into the narrative framework takes two main forms. The first and most common form is that of interaction through a character representing the player. Players can thus see themselves virtualized on the screen as a sexy female archeologist (*Tomb Raider*), a hero of the Niebelungen (*Ring*), or a California detective (*Blade Runner*), to mention only a few examples from what is a constantly developing field. But players can also interact directly with the virtual environment, their presence registered on the screen as an empty space without mass or reflection but nevertheless capable of moving about, manipulating objects, opening notebooks, and even being the passive addressee of an actor in the story (*Myst, Riven*). In these games, the reader does not create the story, and the movements and actions triggered by mouse clicks are clearly limited to the possibilities provided in the algorithms of the program. The illusion of freedom of action is quite strong, however, because of the fact that the choices are not offered verbally, which substantially reduces the player's analytical capacities.

Here we are clearly no longer dealing with a text in the traditional sense. But it would be difficult to maintain that there is no reading, since players actively interpret signs, decode configurations, make choices based on clues they collect, and produce meaning by relating information to an initial context. Just as in traditional novels, in which actions and descriptive pauses alternate, readers of a hyperfiction are led by a tightly linked narrative chain and a desire to "know what comes next," while occasionally pausing to contemplate the images offered to them. We can thus call these works pseudo-texts, a concept that will here designate any nonlinguistic object whose configuration lends itself to the operations of reading. More precisely, a pseudo-text is a set of information of a certain scope that may be read by a person with the skills needed to identify the main information and apprehend it in a meaningful way by means of various cognitive activities, such as establishing relationships, making a selection, or recalling a previous event. From this perspective, a building is a pseudo-text for an architect, just as a painting is for a painter, because these professionals are able to see in them the choices made by their creators and establish relationships among their various parts. As with text, the greater the skills of the reader, the richer a pseudo-text will be. I thus fully agree with Gadamer, for whom there is reading not only of texts, but also of visual art and buildings, since reading is the fundamental mode of the encounter with art. We shall come back to this question in the section "Reading Images."

The interactive revolution lies in this apparently limitless extension of the processes of reading far beyond the verbal matter in which they have specialized for several thousand years, particularly since the advent of printing. Thanks to interactivity, reading is now able to address nonverbal signs, which can be made perfectly operational through the use of conventions within a closed environment.

15

Varieties of Hypertext

In computer science, the concept of hypertext designates a way of making direct connections among various pieces of information, textual or nontextual, that may or may not be located in the same file (or on the same "page") by means of embedded links. Using an interface based primarily on visual and intuitive elements such as color and icons, hypertext users can identify the places in a document where additional information is attached and access them directly with a mouse click.

Literary theory also uses the term *hypertext*, but in a very different sense. For Gérard Genette, for example, hypertext is "any text derived from a previous text either through simple transformation . . . or through indirect transformation."[1] In this sense, James Joyce's *Ulysses* is a hypertext of Homer's *Odyssey*. The current concept of hypertext, as it comes to us from computer science and the Web, is closer to that of intertext as first proposed by Julia Kristeva and redefined by Michael Riffaterre: "the perception, by the reader, of a relationship between a work and others that have either preceded or followed it."[2] But the two concepts do not coincide completely, since the intertext, in this meaning, results from the act of reading, while the hypertext we are talking about is a computer construct of links and data corresponding to files or parts of files that can be displayed in windows of various dimensions.

There are many hypertext software programs. Among the pioneers are Hypercard, Hyperties, KMS, Intermedia, and Notecards. Since the advent of the Web, hypertext has been based mainly on HTML (HyperText Markup Language), XML (Extensible Markup Language), and XHTML.

Historically, the term *hypertext* was created in 1965 by Ted Nelson, who used it to designate a new way of writing on the computer, in which the units of text could be accessed nonsequentially. The text thus created would reproduce the nonlinear structure of ideas as opposed to the "linear" format of books, films, or speech. Nelson himself was indebted to a visionary article by Vannevar Bush, who in 1945 already envisaged a huge storage system for human knowledge that anyone would be able to connect to and that would allow them to annotate documents of interest. Even before the introduction of the personal computer, Nelson had attempted to realize Bush's dream using a computer system called Xanadu—the name of Mongol emperor Kublai Khan's palace, immortalized in a poem by Coleridge as a symbol of memory and its accumulated treasures. Nelson's Xanadu was supposed to lead to a huge universal library system (docuverse), which could be consulted on workstations by making "micropayments" for each information node accessed. Despite its commercial implications, Nelson's model had a profound influence on the evolution of hypertext, and the World Wide Web may be seen as its culmination in an unrestricted form.

Hypertext can be used to manipulate data of all kinds, not only linguistic data but also images, sound, video, and animation. It makes it possible to regulate a reader's interaction with a document by programming various behavior into objects on the screen in relation to the reader's movements of the mouse: the author of a computer program can stipulate, for example, that touching a certain word with the mouse pointer will change its form or color or trigger a process that will lead to a new text. Through these features, hypertext creates a radically new form of electronic dialogue in written language. Even more numerous than the many forms of books, hypertext products vary substantially in appearance and internal organization. Indeed, computer technology can give digitized text any form imaginable.

In a text on paper, the paragraphs or blocks of information are arranged in sequence, and the reader can access them essentially through contiguity, relying on a number of tabular elements. In a hypertext, the various blocks of information may be distinct and autonomous and may be located on a single "page" or on separate "pages." In accordance with the nature of the document and the target readers, the author of a hypertext can provide access by means of selection, association, contiguity, or stratification, and these modes can exist alone or in different combinations.

> *Selection.* In the simplest case, selection, readers select the block of information they want to read from a list or enter a letter on the keyboard. The various blocks of information are distinct units with no essential links among them. Readers are guided by a specific need for information, which exists only until it is satisfied. This model is

typical of the catalogue, the entire organization of which is based on the principle of expansion, with each word of the index leading to a detailed description. Dictionaries also work on this principle, but each of their entries can also contain references to other entries such as synonyms, antonyms, and so on. The user may also select from the list of pages already consulted in the document during the work session or may choose from a table of contents or from a tree diagram in which the various branchings are accessible at different hierarchical levels. Finally, the most frequent mode of selection is by means of hyperlinks indicated by a particular color, on which the user clicks in order to explore the content behind them.

Applied to a text of a certain scope, the principle of selection is also characteristic of hypertext fiction in which each screen page includes several links to other pages, making Jorge Luis Borges's ideal of forking paths a reality. Similarly, in the case of a philosophical essay, every block of text could be followed by a number of icons, each one corresponding to a possible continuation of the text according to the anticipated reactions of the reader insofar as the author could predict them. After reading a segment of text, the reader could select the most relevant continuation. In so doing, he or she would become actively involved in reading, making choices, and expressing opinions at every step through each section read. But the number of combinations can easily skyrocket. If a block of text gives rise to three choices, and each of these gives rise to another three, there would be nine possible continuations of the initial text at the third level, twenty-seven at the fourth level, and eighty-one at the fifth. As a result, 121 texts would have to be written for a sequence of five paragraphs to be accessible in perfectly "free" hypertext mode. Thus the idea of providing choices at every level has to be abandoned, or their proliferation would lead the reader into endless movement and force the author to rigorously explore every logical alternative at each point in the argument. Moreover, the freedom given the reader is purely artificial; it only reinforces the dominant position of the author, who is the master of all possible outcomes.

Selection and association. In this mode, readers choose the element they wish to consult but can also navigate among the blocks of information, letting themselves be guided by the associations of ideas that arise as they navigate and by the links offered them. This model is typical of encyclopedias.

Selection, association, and contiguity. In addition to the above-mentioned modes of navigation, the blocks of information are here accessible sequentially, like the pages of a book. This model is suitable for an essay or a scientific article and would be used, for example, for adaptations of printed books. It corresponds to a simple transposition of codex format to electronic format. For example, in a hypertext adaptation of an essay such as Marvin Minsky's *Society of Mind*, readers can choose to select a title in the table of contents, search for a word in the index, or move from section to section by scrolling. The contiguity mode is useful only if a document is divided into pages and sections that are supposed to be read in a specific order—as is usually the case with a book.

Selection, association, contiguity, and stratification. In addition to being accessible by the above-mentioned modes, the elements of information can be distributed in two or three hierarchical levels according to their degree of complexity. This makes it possible to meet the needs of various categories of readers or to satisfy different information needs for a single reader. This hypertext model best combines the advantages of the codex with the possibilities opened up by the computer by taking into account a new dimension of the text, that of depth. By superimposing different layers of text on a single subject, or to use another metaphor, by encircling a central nucleus with various supplementary documents, the uses of which are well defined, a stratified hypertext provides several books in one.

Users of such a hypertext could scroll through pages in a main window, while at the same time being able to open one or more secondary windows, providing more theoretical or more popularized discourse. There are many fields in which this type of structure with two or three layers, offering a basic discourse and additional windows accessible on demand, is desirable. This is the case for self-teaching textbooks and learning situations, for example, in which the learner is confronted with a mass of interrelated concepts that may not all be familiar. It is also the case for technical manuals in which the user may at any time want to consult supplementary information on a specific element.

These four modes of navigation may also be combined in the electronic edition of a work, opening up new perspectives for critical editions of works on paper. The main thread of reading would thus be the final version of the text, dominating the layers of the previous versions, which the reader could also choose to display in parallel windows. The different pages of the text would be accessed by contiguity or by selection in a table of contents. Finally, comments, notes, and illustrations would be accessible through connections or associative links. Because of the richness and diversity of the links provided, I will call this ideal type of hypertext a "stratified" or "tabular" hypertext.

The success of a tool of this kind obviously depends on the consistency and interest of the base layer. While this is relatively easy to determine in the case of a critical edition, the same is not true for other documents. In a textbook aimed at a diverse readership, the various strata of information it should contain would have to be established. The base layer would contain the main thread of the text, consisting of the minimum information at a medium level of difficulty. On every page where needed, hyperlinks would open one or two supplementary windows, such as a "novice" window for users whose knowledge is insufficient for them to grasp the main ideas and an "expert" window for those who already possess the basic knowledge and want to know more.

In creating an arrangement capable of working in depth and not only on the surface of the thread of discourse, the author of a tabular hypertext must take the utmost care in establishing the different layers and distributing the information between the base level and the other layers. These choices will vary with the type of text and target audience. The levels of information may be distributed on the axis of concrete/abstract or divided between narrative and documents or between scholarly text, experimental data, and reference works, or between didactic text, examples, and exercises, and so on.

Generally speaking, it does not seem desirable to create more than two layers in addition to the base level. Increasing the number of layers will result in a proliferation of cross-references, and reading would quickly become difficult. It is important to remember that in a reader-based textual economy, reference markers should be provided that allow readers to predict the results of their actions when moving the mouse pointer over the surface of the screen. The presence of a "novice" or an "expert" layer linked to a particular word or page should thus always be indicated in the same way, by an icon or the use of a color. Novice readers who click on an icon hoping to find an explanation at their level would quickly become discouraged if, instead of getting what they wanted, they encountered material intended for experts. To be effective, reading must be based on stable conventions that enable maximum concentration on the content.

Stratified hypertext will undoubtedly develop its own conventions just as the print media did, and these will become part of readers' culture. In spite of the problems, this is where the most promising future for hypertext lies if it is to move beyond the stage of utopian dreams of liberation to become a productive working tool. However, these modes of organization of hypertext may lead to methods of navigation that are very different depending on the degree of opacity or tabularity of the presentation of data. A literary or game hypertext may opt for greater opacity in navigation and allow users to produce events on the screen without knowing where they are or where they are going. In this case, there are no obvious "movements," since everything occurs within the same visual framework. This form of opaque hypertext may be suited to an experimental narrative such as Stuart Moulthrop's *Hegirascope*[3] or to an adventure game such as *Myst*, in which the players have no idea of their position in relation to the puzzles to be solved. For an informational document, however, the most satisfying option for readers is one that gives them a clear view of the distribution of information and enables them to directly access all the blocks, with full control of their movement. In this regard, it is significant that some games allow players to choose the episode they want and allow them to display the percentage of the episode completed at any time.

One area where the user's route cannot be left to chance is learning. Instructional programs and textbooks are based precisely on the principle that the acquisition of knowledge cannot take place in random order guided only by the learner's associations. The first computer-assisted learning (CAL) programs took this principle of the sequential path to the limit, locking students into programmed paths in which access to each exercise was conditional on success in the previous one. Students were expected to move forward blindly, without knowing how many steps they would have to go through or even, sometimes, what they would actually learn from the program. Hypertext, too, can be used in an opaque manner, to totally control users' progress, allowing them to follow only branchings accepted by the logic of the program, thus reinforcing traditional practices of computer-assisted learning. I believe, however, that hypertext should adopt some of the characteristics of the age-old technology of the book to create a new product that will satisfy the needs of demanding readers who use it as a tool for informational or educational purposes.

As we can see, the production of a hypertext requires constant strategic choices by the author. The distribution of elements of information also poses the problem of identifying every primary textual unit with a title. If these titles are meaningful to the users, it will be easier for them not only to find the information they want, but also to keep track of which pages they have read when they exit from the hypertext. In this way, readers will be able to have real control over the text instead of being controlled by it or groping their way through it.

16

Context and Hypertext

In the early nineties, hypertext creators and theorists such as Michael Joyce, Stuart Moulthrop, and J. Yellowlees Douglas envisioned an extraordinary convergence between new technology and postmodern literary theory. George P. Landow, the most important theorist on this front, stated, "Electronic linking, which provides one of the defining features of hypertext, also embodies Julia Kristeva's notion of intertextuality, Mikhail Bakhtin's emphasis upon multivocality, Michel Foucault's conception of networks of power, and Gilles Deleuze and Félix Guattari's ideas of rhizomatic, nomad thought."[1] According to this widely accepted view, of which Eastgate.com was the standard bearer, literary hypertext should aim to radically distinguish itself from the traditional novel by not imposing a fixed sequence on the reader's path. Readers would click on links leading to new blocks of information, following only their own associative network, wandering in total freedom. To open up this space for the readers' clicks, hypertext fiction would necessarily have to be cut up into segments connected by a network of hyperlinks, among which readers would navigate as they wished, preferably in an opaque manner, not following any imposed order.

Such an idyllic view of reading assumed that the author of a hypertext would, for all intents and purposes, refrain from manipulating the reader's context of reception—which would be tantamount to committing artistic hara-kiri. On the basis of this dogmatic view, hypertext enthusiasts in the early nineties were segmenting all kinds of documents to adapt them to the new medium. For example, Vannevar Bush's groundbreaking article was "hypertextualized" into seven numbered sections that could be accessed in any order.

It is not at all certain, however, that readers have anything to gain from such an operation of dismemberment, because it displaces the problem of creating the context and the connections among the fragments, which is normally the author's job. Readers confronting a series of fragments would thus have to first find a context according to which to interpret the data in order to satisfy their demand for meaning.

Reading hypertext is thus not a self-sustaining process, unlike reading traditional text, in which the connections between paragraphs and chapters are planned by the author and are sometimes the result of highly refined strategies for creating expectations. These strategies begin with the first lines and even the title pages (book title, chapter titles) and the paratext in general, whose function is precisely to guide the patterns of reception and create networks through which everything that follows will have meaning. A chapter may include an epigraph that readers will want to relate to the following text. Or the narrator may announce at the beginning that a spicy story will be told, which may be revealed bit by bit in the course of the narrative or whose final outcome may never be fully revealed, as in *Tristram Shandy.* Thus, the organization of the book and the thread of the text constantly push the narrative forward, and readers are invited to follow it until they attain the promised knowledge or accept its absence, which inevitably occurs at the very end.

Lacking this promise of revelation in the narrative thread, readers of fragments constantly have to clear the contents of their immediate memory, reject the cognitive markers they had identified in reading the previous fragment, and recreate a context of reception that is suitable for the new fragment. This process of repeated decontextualization leads to a risk of fatigue. What is the point of continuing to click on words when one has absolutely no idea what type of text they are going to lead to? Without adequate ongoing stimulation, the initial impetus of the reader's quest is destined to be quickly exhausted.

The author of a hypertext can, however, guide the reader's navigation by providing clues about the content of the page to which a particular link leads. Giving each page or each fragment a title can help create a context of reception. But at the same time, it weakens the illusion of continuity from one fragment to the next and can undermine the reading context that has been established.

Regardless of the method used, hypertext cannot establish a new way of reading without the incentive of freedom of choice. This is already provided in newspapers, which on the surface of a single or double page offer a choice of ten or twenty different texts that the eye may select, snatch in passing, absorb in fragments, or sometimes abandon barely begun. But newspapers have the advantage of a space large enough to fill the reader's entire visual span. In contrast, the computer screen, with its limited surface area, cannot offer the eye large numbers of columns of information or photographs: it has to appeal to readers by other means. A hypertext thus has to be carefully designed to create the equivalent of a rich and diverse type layout. The basic rule is to use small characters when providing a substantial mass of text, and to segment the screen into specialized areas so that readers constantly have navigation markers and can conduct their reading activity in a tabular fashion, choosing among the various elements of a mosaic. This is what is done in newspapers and magazines.

Another general principle is to constantly renew the incentives used to maintain the reader's interest. In a work of media art, every click on a button, every change of page creates a new "event": a short sound clip, a pop-up image, the opening of a window, a change in the typographic attributes of a text, the movement of an iconic or textual element—anything that attracts attention. The possibilities are limited only by the graphic designer's imagination. The more varied the events and the more relevant they are to the subject of the hypertext, the more lively, interactive, and captivating the space of the screen will be for the reader.[2] This spectacularization of the text shows the power of the computer as a "writing/reading machine."

17

The Limitations of Lists

One way to limit the effects of decontextualization in a hypertext is to place the links in a list. The list is the archetypal form of hypertext writing; it was handled perfectly by HTML and was the most widespread genre of discourse in the early years of the Web. This represents a curious return to the past, as the list is as ancient as writing itself. According to anthropologist Jack Goody, it emerged with the very first systems of writing and was widely used as early as 3000 BCE. The Sumerians used three main types of lists: (1) the retrospective list, for events, social roles, persons; (2) the inventory list, for actions to be carried out and checked off as they were done; (3) the lexical list, the embryonic form of our dictionaries.

What characterizes lists is that their information is not presented analogically in relation to speech, using verbal textual connections, but rather in a form specific to writing, based on the visual realm and tabularity. As Goody observes, the list contrasts with the connectedness characteristic of oral discourse: "The list relies on discontinuity rather than continuity."[1] It thus changed writing by providing "a locational sorting device."[2] Since hypertext writing is very well suited to these characteristics of the list, it is not surprising that this form is so popular on the Web. Consisting of autonomous elements generally a single line in length, lists also have the advantage of being easy to read on the screen. Finally, since they bring together elements belonging to the same class, they make it possible to avoid the problem of decontextualization discussed above, which is the blind spot of hypertext. It is this affinity of hypertext with lists that, for example, allows a grandmother to produce, for her grandchildren and for Internet users throughout the world, a Web page listing all the games she knows, grouped in categories—card games, word games, and the like—in which each item of the list leads to a site devoted to that particular game. The most characteristic writing of our modern period thus revives a form invented some five thousand years ago between the Tigris and the Euphrates by people who had discovered the usefulness of recording the information they considered most worth preserving on sun-dried clay tablets.

In order to avoid the dullness of an ordered list, it is possible to adopt a spatial representation in which the elements are grouped by semantic field or positioned in the form of a map. Visual effects can also be produced by arranging the elements in a nonlinear order and linking them in a visual thread in order to metaphorically suggest a path for the reader to follow.

Despite all these advantages, the list is the true "degree zero" of text, in the sense that it neither constrains nor supports reading as textual syntax can. This is because the elements of a list are not syntactically linked, but are simply juxtaposed. Lists can therefore accommodate only items pertaining to the same class or that are related hierarchically. Lists may be used to comic effect, and Rabelais, for example, abundantly exploited the humorous potential of lengthy enumerations. But lists are not capable of expressing the sometimes very subtle relationships indicated by the many coordinating or subordinating connectives: relationships of cause ("since," "because," "as," etc.), of condition ("if," "provided that," etc.), of opposition and concession ("but," "although," "despite," "rather," etc.), of consequence ("therefore," "so that," etc.), of time ("when," "as soon as," etc.), of purpose ("in order to," "so as to," etc.), of transition ("and yet," "thus," etc.), of comparison ("like," "as," etc.), of restriction ("however," etc.), and others. It is these connectives that provide all the richness of an argument and make it possible to communicate nuanced, complex cognitive configurations to a reader. Lacking them, lists can function only as raw information, without any possibility of developing a complex discourse or creating a narrative universe.

18

Aporias of Hyperfiction

Actually, there is no story for which the question
"How does it continue?" would not be legitimate.
—Walter Benjamin, "The Storyteller"

If we examine hyperfictions from the point of view of the reading process required, we observe a large variety of genres, differentiated according to certain parameters: the degree of control given to the reader, the nature of the texts, and the importance of the visual. The first hyperfictions forced readers to navigate blindly. This is the case, for example, for Michael Joyce's *afternoon, a story*, which a *New York Times* critic hailed as anticipating the novel of the future.[1] In this narrative, which comprises 539 fragments and 950 hyperlinks, readers have almost no control over the path of their reading. Not only do they not know which segment of the novel they are looking at, but they have no way to reread a passage they have already read in a previous session. In addition, certain passages can be accessed only after a specific textual sequence has been visited. These characteristics were obviously intended by the author and are not inherent to the computer medium. As Michael Joyce subsequently explained in a discussion of this type of experiment: "I wanted, quite simply, to write a novel that would change in successive readings and to make those changing versions according to the connections that I had for some time naturally discovered in the process of writing and that I wanted my readers to share."[2]

Other hyperfictions provide a more obvious unifying thread when they are organized around common metaphors. In *Trip*, by Matthew Miller (1996), navigation is based on a map of the United States: Readers click on one of the states on the map to discover and follow the thread of the narrative. In *My Body* (1997), Shelley Jackson uses a sketch of a female body to call up autobiographical memories.[3] The stories provided are often very brief—a few lines or a few screens. But with the inclusion of images in a barely suggested narrative framework, some of them succeed in creating an effect that is enigmatic and poetic.[4]

Many hyperfictions of this period are essentially essays on hypertext and dwell on the question of the importance that will be placed on reading. The most readable texts are those that function on the basis of cognitively provocative aphorisms or paradoxes, such as Stuart Moulthrop's *Hegirascope* (1995–1997),[5] which consists of 175 pages and 700 hyperlinks. Unlike the first version of this essay, the current one now goes automatically to the next page after thirty seconds of inactivity, but readers can always move through the labyrinth as they wish.

HyperWeb, by Adrian Miles,[6] which dates from 1996, not only uses language but also gives visual symbolism an important place. Each page is de-

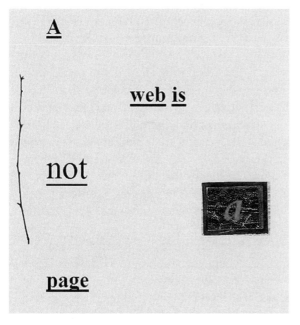

In Adrian Miles's *HyperWeb*, the pages load automatically one after another, providing the reader with a poetic and pictorial meditation on hypertext (http://vogmae.net .au/works/hyperweb/2_148 .html).

signed as a visual unit incorporating illustrations and aphoristic sentences ("A web is not a page," "A web is not a tree"); it is more like a poem or a calligram than a work of fiction. It should be noted that, as in the Moulthrop work, the pages load automatically one after another, although readers can also click on links in elements of the text or the illustrations. This type of directed linear reading was probably considered necessary in order to lead readers through a textual continuum, at least until a sufficient reception context was created for reading to be propelled by its own movement. Instead of indicating the number of screen pages, the introduction tells readers that the automatic cycling of the pages takes six to seven minutes. In these examples, the activity involved is closer to watching a show than to reading a book, not so much because of the importance placed on the visual as because of the reader's lack of control over the turning of the pages.

More than ten years after the discovery of the new narrative space opened up by hypertext, the question of whether it is possible to reproduce in this format a reading experience comparable to that provided by the great novels remains unresolved. The novel has long been the genre most suited to continuous reading, but it is not yet certain that it can be transplanted to the computer screen. (This subject is explored further in the section "The Decline of the Novel.")

There is no doubt that hypertext fiction possesses all the syntactic, visual, and interactive resources needed to engage users in experiences of extended immersion in imaginary universes. But the most successful achievements in this field have been in games rather than reading. In games, users are concerned not with enriching their worldview through imaginary contact with other inner universes, but rather with manipulating objects and characters, improving their motor skills, competing in using weapons and other objects on the screen, solving puzzles, or earning points by completing a set course. Even in the hyperfictions cited above, readers are less occupied in reading than in clicking on links. For this reason, Espen Aarseth proposes that these works be called ergodic literature,[7] a category that includes works as diverse as the *I Ching*, Queneau's *Cent mille milliards de poèmes* (1961) (translated as *One Hundred Million Million Poems* [1983]), and adventure games of the MUD (multiuser dungeon) type.

It is certainly possible to imagine hypertexts with a narrative thread that would be essentially based on language and that would opt for tabularity rather than opaque or labyrinthic navigation. A tabular hypernarrative would, by my definition, be one that provided readers with multiple entry points, so that they could quickly find or return to elements that interested them. In addition to being divided into chapters and having a table of contents, it might have a thematic index (like those already found in such works as *Life: A User's Manual*, by Georges Perec), a general map of places visited (as in fantasy novels such as Tolkien's *Lord of the Rings*), a list of the characters and their relationships (as in plays), a chronology of events, and so on. By clicking on a place on the map, readers would be able to see a display of references to the different passages of the narrative that took place there. They could also quickly locate all passages dealing with a particular theme, which could either be tagged in advance by the author or found through a search using an indexing engine. With some types of narrative, readers could also navigate using quotations or illustrations that would lead them to the corresponding text. Finally, one can imagine readers having access to all the glosses or commentaries on passages of a work, such as is found in databases of films or large bookstores. One can find an example of this mode of structure in the CD-ROM *Red Planet*, which was thought of, according to its authors, as the "equivalent of a book, that is, as a thesis-driven work of original scholarship."[8]

Actually, it seems quite difficult to initiate a strong, sustained reading process if everything depends on chance clicks and if readers do not feel constrained by a necessary and unavoidable course of events. The reading contract implicit in the novel excludes readers' interference with the events they witness. Reading a story means encountering something that already exists, an intangible past. People listening to a story told orally also have no control over the events recounted. There is nothing we can do to allow Oedipus to escape his fate. A hero whose actions were directed by the reader would no longer be a hero, but a puppet, an abstraction devoid of depth or density, incapable of moving us. It is the weight of necessity, of fate, that drives our emotional reactions and makes us weep for Antigone or Fabrice Del Dongo. The ending may have been decided arbitrarily by the author, as Benjamin has noted, but the reader has no way of escaping it, and that is part of the contract.

Looking back on fifteen years of experiments in hypertext fiction from the point of view of both writer and reader, Tim Parks makes a rather negative assessment of the field. According to him, the fundamental question about the genre is the literary value of the much-vaunted freedom the new medium gives readers to control the course of their reading. This, he points out, is not the primary function of reading: "When I read another's work it is to confront a different vision from my own, not to steer it to familiar destinations."[9] In addition to the fact that hypertext fiction cannot give readers the sense of reaching a satisfactory conclusion, Parks notes that the inclusion of all sorts of visual or sound effects in the text tends to detract from the role of language. This criticism brings us back to the problem discussed above, the conflict between meaning and effect, which is a result of our cognitive architecture; as soon as the effects become too pervasive, they monopolize all attention and relegate meaning to second place.

Another drawback of the hyperfictions written in the wake of Joyce's *afternoon, a story* is their reliance on the principle that navigation should be opaque to the reader and based in large measure on random choices. This seems quite contrary to the common motivation for reading. People read not only to pass the time or to find meaning, but to be part of a community of readers and to share experiences. To do so, they make annotations, they discuss passages with their friends, or they reread passages years later, reinterpreting them in light of the context or subsequent readings. By excluding these possibilities, the current model of hyperfiction deprives itself of what is in fact the main asset of the computer and information technology: the ability to easily exchange comments on texts, as people do in blogs, for example (see chapter 38, "The Rise of the Blog"). There is thus more truth than J. Yellowlees Douglas anticipated in her comment that "If the book is a highly refined example of a primitive technology, hypertext is a primitive example of a highly refined technology."[10]

19

Reading Images

The pictures that make up our world are symbols,
signs, messages and allegories. Or perhaps they are
merely empty presences that we fill with our desire,
experience, questioning and regret.

—Alberto Manguel, *Reading Pictures*

Although the concept of reading has been substantially broadened in recent decades, it is no exaggeration to say that it may still be seen as an operation with two components. The first component, which belongs to the realm of perception, is carried out by the visual apparatus—or by touch, for books in Braille—and consists in gathering the characters or words of a piece of writing or a given code from an appropriate surface. The other component of the operation is cognitive and involves the semiotic processing of the elements perceived. This presupposes that the characters or words involved are organized coherently to enable a reading that can be reproduced and shared with a community.

Why should the senses involved in the first component of reading be limited to those of sight and touch? Wouldn't it be reasonable to include hearing, since blind people use audio recordings? Even though the minicassette has become established as a medium for the book, it remains an indirect one. What is recorded is not written language, but sound. One does not read an audiotape; one can only listen to it. The difference between the two activities is crucial. Sound is by nature transitory. It exists only while it is being produced; it cannot be fixed in a given moment. Oral language thus belongs to the flow of time. In contrast, what belongs to the domain of the eye can be stopped and manipulated at will. It is possible at any time, without using any particular technology, to go backward in a text, to isolate segments and hold them in one's gaze, to relate them to other segments or establish hierarchies among them, to place markers, to make annotations, or to indicate paths. Sight is the ideal sense for intellection, since it permits the unlimited analysis of the data being considered. Hearing, in contrast, captures the entire mass of sound present at a given time—although the brain can learn to neutralize ambient noise—and it can do so only if it does not fix it, but follows it in its temporal movement. Hence the world of sound is not normally the object of reading, since that operation requires a control over the data that hearing cannot provide. Moreover, the world of the visible is not reducible to the world of the readable, but extends far beyond it, since not everything we see demands or lends itself to reading.

Nor should reading be limited to linguistic material only, since it is quite possible to read things other than text. For example, we learn to read graphs, charts, diagrams, plans, and maps. In these examples, the operation of reading is recognizable by the fact that it is necessary to establish relations between coded data in order to produce meaning—whether these data involve variations in the height of a curve on the x-axis in relation to the y-axis, the distance between points, the thickness of bars, variations in color, or symbols used to designate natural or cultural phenomena. These expanded meanings of the verb *read* are widely accepted, to the point that the ability to read diagrams is now included in textbooks teaching reading.

The concept of reading entails high-level cognitive operations involving what an individual knows and what he or she is. Someone who claims to have read a book is supposed to have assimilated it, at least to some extent. In contrast, simply looking at it involves little intellectual activity, and even less in the case of a purely tactile operation ("I leafed through it"). These actions belong to perception more than to cognition and expose us only superficially to patterns produced by the text.

Everyday language has two different verbs to designate vision, differentiated according to whether the person is passive or active. The verb *to see* describes someone experiencing a sight that is before his or her eyes and corresponds to passive reception; the verb *to look* describes a more active, more attentive position and implies a certain concentration of the gaze, a focus on a given area. The art scholar E. H. Gombrich has observed that "reading shows our capacity of information-processing at its most mysterious."[1] And it is true that the act of reading involves maximum visual concentration. The verb *to read* can be applied to an action only if certain conditions are met. It implies not only the concentration of the gaze but also the controlled performance of a certain number of specific intellectual operations. Reading implies an intentional act of perception of signs that exist in the realm of the gaze—or its equivalent for the visually impaired—and are subject to ordered processing. The three verbs under consideration here are thus not interchangeable, for we certainly do not *read* everything we *look at* and, still less, everything we *see*. We would normally hesitate to say, for example, that we are planning to go "read" the paintings in a museum, since paintings are first and foremost surfaces that must be apprehended globally by the eye, or simply "seen," in order to be "looked at." The verb *to read*, however, is increasingly used here as well, especially in the infinitive, in technical or scholarly contexts when there is a desire to emphasize the semiotic processing of the image and to apply the active procedures of attention and production of meaning usually reserved for written material. For example, the semiologist of the image Louis Marin, in a discussion of Poussin's *Israelites Gathering the Manna*, demonstrated that we can "read a picture," an activity that involves "both . . . discerning what elements in the picture constitute signs, and . . . stating, declaring what these signs signify."[2] Gadamer also takes the view that we can read works of visual art, and even buildings: "I feel strongly that reading, and not reproduction, is the real mode of experience of the work of art and the one that defines it as such. We are talking here about reading in the 'eminent' meaning of the term. . . . Any encounter with art occurs essentially through reading. There is reading not only of texts, but also of paintings and buildings."[3]

For anyone who fully accepts the possibility of reading images, there will be a great temptation to put into operation a "reading machine" that would be as effective for this type of material as for text. This is what Barthes seems to have had in mind in *Camera Lucida*. Initially overwhelmed by "the disorder which from the very first I had observed in Photography," he felt he had suddenly discovered a "structural rule" to explain why certain photographs held his gaze while others left him indifferent.[4] This rule involves finding in a photograph "the co-presence of two discontinuous elements, heterogeneous," which he calls the *studium* and the *punctum*. The studium corresponds to the photographer's intentions as Barthes identifies them in the photograph, while the punctum is the detail that holds the viewer's attention and that, not necessarily intentionally, attracts his or her gaze and perhaps even mobilizes it entirely: Andy Warhol's dirty fingernails, someone's crossed arms, an aide-de-camp in a kilt beside Queen Victoria, or the texture of a paving stone.

Anyone examining photographs in light of these comments cannot fail to recognize a certain truth in this analysis. Following the great critic, they too will be able to discover the significant interplay of studium and punctum here and there and will study photographs by concentrating on some detail that may give them a special meaning transcending the intentions of their author. If we look more closely, however, we will finally be forced to admit that the meaning thus obtained is highly subjective, and that we could have obtained others by using a different division of the elements arbitrarily defined as studium and punctum.

In my view, Barthes's approach aimed to transpose to the world of images the mechanism that has proven so effective when applied to text, a kind of two-phase machine, as we have seen, involving, in the first phase, establishing an appropriate context—the theme, or studium—against which a significant detail—the rheme, or punctum—is then examined. This process may appear particularly legitimate to a literate person, since it is based on the way we commonly read, whether we are dealing with the basic structure of a sentence or with the relationship between a text and the title attached to it or between an image and its caption.

A painting is perceived as a totality from the first look; it is then possible for the viewer to select any detail to place against the background of the whole. Each such instance of establishing a relationship can produce a different reading, and therefore a different meaning, determined by the viewer. This is equally true of hypertext, which does not in principle present any necessary beginning or end to the various reading paths available—except that the mode of expression is profoundly different, and that in the painting all the elements are present simultaneously, whereas in hypertext they are placed in a relationship of reciprocal substitution.

But make no mistake, reading an image, in the fullest sense of the word, will give rise to a feeling of completion and necessity only insofar as it is carried out on a narrative sequence or on the relationship of such a sequence to a meaningful caption. The most typical example is that of allegorical works, which take on their full meaning only with their title, such as the painting *The Israelites Gathering the Manna* analyzed by Louis Marin. But Marin, the semiologist of the image, was not taken in by the metaphor implicit in such operations of reading; he recognized elsewhere that language and painting do not signify in the same way. As he stated incisively, "In language, ideas substitute for signs so that minds can communicate. In painting, signs substitute for things so that imaginations can be delighted."[5]

Sartre, too, contrasted the semiotic functioning of images with that of linguistic signs: "The painter is mute. He presents you with *a* hovel, that's all. You are free to see in it what you like. That attic window will never be a symbol of misery; for that, it would have to be a sign, whereas it is a thing."[6] Unlike myth, which according to Lévi-Strauss always has at least the function of "signifying signification," an image can simply "be there," or it can be invested with symbolic value according to the relationship a person has with it. Thus we can say with Régis Debray that the image is "forever and definitively enigmatic, without any possible *good lesson*. It has five billion potential versions (as many as there are human beings), none of which is authoritative (the author's no more than any other)."[7]

Without going as far as Lyotard, for whom "A scene is not read; it is not understood,"[8] it must nonetheless be recognized that the operation of reading should in the case of a painting normally be invested with a weaker meaning than in the case of a text. There may indeed be reading, that is, an activity of deciphering/interpretation in which the gaze scans the picture's surface to identify differences and continuities, but in comparison to text, the signifying matter of a painting is not only difficult to identify with certainty but is irremediably inert, often lacking any narrative movement or syntactic mechanism that would sustain the operation of reading and the production of meaning. A semiotics of the image may well identify topological relationships of neighboring, separation, encasing, envelopment, order of succession, and vectoriality, as proposed by Fernande Saint-Martin.[9] But since images have no linear organization or codified syntax, viewers cannot know where to start or stop collecting significant features or in what order to establish their relationships.

Above all, the image does not necessarily require decoding. We know that a person can see an image in a familiar place day after day without paying the least attention to it, without even identifying its theme or subject or remembering ever seeing it, while another person will immediately discover all kinds of significations in it. Here we see the essential difference between text and image: While the former is always a sign for anyone who knows how to read, the latter is silent and does not set in motion a process of reading unless it is appropriately contextualized in its immediate environment—as in the case of advertising—through the richness of the emotions, through the "encyclopedia" it calls up in viewers, or through the significant oppositions upon which it is constructed. Since there is no code, it does not trigger any process of active decoding in those perceiving it, as reading does; as we know, once the reading mechanism has been acquired by a child, it tends to begin automatically when any text appears in the field of vision. As Gombrich observes, "pictures don't tell their own story."[10] A painting does not express itself in statements; it does not speak. Whereas the text excels at stimulating the production of meaning—and takes shape only in the movement of reading—the image is merely there, striking us suddenly or leaving us indifferent. It is thus always closer to raw sensation, to the realm of nature and of the nonmechanizable. It seduces, impresses, suggests, and it sometimes incites the viewer to stop and explore or contemplate, but it does not supply the keys that will be sure to engage the process of signification.

Even advertising images, when they communicate a message, do so mainly through their intentionality, the products with which they are associated, and their verbal environment. Their interest does not lie primarily in a structure of meaning with which they can be equated but in the emotional effect they may produce in viewers. In this regard, it is significant that so cerebral a painter as Magritte held the view that "the meaning of an image . . . does not reside in the explanation that might be given of it, but in the effect the image produces upon the recipient."[11] It is this necessary opposition between meaning and effect that, in my view, best defines the specificity of the image. Language produces first and foremost meaning (or nonmeaning: nonsense) and secondarily an effect; an image produces an effect (or a noneffect) and secondarily meaning.

Films, like speech, present a sequence of temporally oriented signs; they disappear as soon as their movement is stopped. Viewers are fascinated by the unfolding action that they cannot interrupt, and they are unable to take any mental distance from what is before their eyes; only afterward will they be able to look back and make connections between what they have seen and what they know—their "encyclopedia," to use Umberto Eco's term.[12] In contrast, reading a text is an activity that can at any moment be deliberately interrupted for reflection. To read a text is to entrust it to our inner silence, where it resonates with the areas of our memory that can best relate to it, shed light on our understanding of it, and be changed by it. Readers can always modulate the rhythm of this activity, speeding it up or slowing it down according to their strategies of comprehension and their intentions.

Live shows, which are also temporally oriented, defy reading even more than films do, because their environment can be much more heterogeneous. Hence it is more difficult to gather signs in order to determine a hierarchy and establish relationships among them. Making a reading would require selecting signs and organizing them in configurations conducive to interpretation—which would inevitably introduce distortions in the initial data. Creators such as Robert Lepage or the Cirque du Soleil excel in using the semiotic overload provided by the environment of a big show to amaze and seduce the modern spectator.

Hypermedia, too, mobilizes something other than the faculties involved in the reading of text. Users do not just need to click on written language in a more or less specific order; they are placed in front of a spectacle combining texts, sounds, colors, images, and animation or video and are solicited from every direction. There is something new, however, in the virtual show in hypermedia that differentiates it from a live show. First, the links among the various elements can be explicit; second, users can control the unfolding of the various components—replay an audio or video document, freeze an image, go backward, or what have you. By bringing the show into the order of the tabular, hypermedia places it under the control of our reading operations, as in the hypertextual multimedia artwork of Ollivier Dyens,[13] for example. But it is especially through the overdetermination of icons or segments of images by placing hyperlinks on them that signs are made to appear and the visible is transformed into the readable.

Various Web sites and virtual magazines explore the many possibilities of combining text, image, and sound in this way, and pioneering projects involving history,[14] visualization of trends,[15] or media arts[16] inspire museums to explore new ways of presenting their collections and contribute to making navigation on the Web an esthetic experience. Insofar as their raw material is visual rather than textual, they avoid the aporias that exist for any work that dismembers the "body of the text" (see chapter 36).

20

The Writer and Images

"A picture is worth a thousand words." This age-old proverb sets the tone, announcing that the relationship between text and image will be one of conflict. There are even some writers who resent the competition of images and express an enduring hatred for them. This was the case for Gustave Flaubert, who in his letters complained repeatedly about the encroachment of illustrations. He saw himself as the most writerly of writers and felt the increasing prominence of images was a threat to the art of the word. In a letter to his friend Georges Charpentier, he stated bluntly that he saw illustrations as a modern invention that dishonored literature.[1] As early as 1862, he rationalized this aversion by denouncing the overly precise nature of images:

> The persistence with which Lévy [his publisher] requests illustrations puts me in a furor that is impossible to describe. . . . Oh! show me the fellow who will do a portrait of Hannibal or a drawing of a Carthaginian chair! he would be doing me a great service. It was hardly worth the trouble to employ such art to leave everything vague so that a boor could come and demolish my dream with his inept precision.
>
> Never while I live will I be illustrated, because: the most beautiful literary description is devoured by the most mediocre drawing. . . . A woman drawn resembles a woman, that is all. The idea is closed, complete, and all the sentences are useless, while a woman written makes one dream of a thousand women.[2]

The debate is an old one. It would be superficial, however, to think that a writer will always put linguistic interests first. Some writers have been fascinated by images. One such is Michel Butor, who has brought painting and language together by working with artists to produce art books. Charles Baudelaire's exclamation in *Mon coeur mis à nu* [My heart laid bare] also comes to mind: "To glorify the cult of images (my great, my only, my primitive passion)."[3]

In fact, these two great art forms speak to us in radically different ways. Text works with meaning and only suggests representations, allowing readers to construct their own images or, more often, to keep them vague. As Jean-Paul Sartre observed: "Writers are agreed that reading is accompanied by few images. In fact, most subjects have few of them and they are also incomplete. . . . the images appear when we cease reading or when our attention begins to wander. But when the reader is engrossed, there are no mental images. . . . A flow of images is characteristic of disturbed and frequently interrupted reading."[4]

Conversely, images present the senses with a vision of an immediate reality, making the work of representation unnecessary. They draw on the support of verbalization only when there is a conscious decision on the part of the viewer. There is only a short step from this observation to the accusation that proponents of the image are intellectually lazy. What lovers of literature criticize in the image is that it seems to give itself as a totality, without the need for any intellectual work. It bears repeating that reading text and reading images call on very different processes.

There are some points of contact between visual and linguistic material, but they are necessarily secondary. In a calligram, for example, the text uses its own visual dimension to produce an image, while remaining in the realm of language: a fine example of hedging one's bets. In the case of a legend, each stays in its own territory, providing an example of cooperation. Etymologically, *legend* means "what is to be read." The term, which was first applied to the lives of saints, later came to also designate what is to be read in an image provided for the reader; the Latin gerundive from which the term originates expresses an obligation.

If an image and a text are placed side by side, which one provides the context for the other? The answer will obviously vary with the nature of the text and of the painting, but it is more likely to be the text. In fact, it is enough to place a phrase beside an image for the image automatically to be seen as an illustration of that phrase—more or less reliable and more or less metaphorical. Even the title of a painting takes priority over the painting itself, as does any title in relation to the text below it. Readers learn very early that, in a book or a newspaper, the purpose of the title is to announce or summarize the text that follows. In painting, as well, we expect the title to translate the quintessence of the painting into the realm of language. Visitors to art museums tend to read the titles of the works exhibited before even beginning to look at them. In other words, the title provides the context for comprehension of the painting; it activates filters in the minds of the readers/viewers that enable them to make the "right" reading and tells them what is to be seen or understood. Since the text is supposed to tell the "truth" about the image, contemporary artists who want to free themselves from this constraint have no choice but to give their works meaningless titles (e.g., "No. 55b") or, like Magritte, who was ahead of his time in this, provocative titles that provide an ironic or paradoxical counterpoint (e.g., "The Treachery of Images") and let the reader play a kind of circular interpretive game, trying to understand the picture according to the legend and vice versa.

In a civilization marked by the increasing prominence of the visual, we can expect a change in this hierarchical relationship of text to image. It is far from certain that coming generations dealing with mixed environments will read the text first, as we so often tend to do. On the contrary, feedback loops will proliferate between text and image, and there will be more influence between them, with the spectacularization of the text fragment and the textualization of the visual. Michel Butor, who was interested in painting and in the increasing prominence of the image in our environment, observed that the most sober newspapers have had to resign themselves to providing space for images. He concluded: "We see before us a new age of text. The text has now been freed from certain constraints, as much as the codex was in relation to the *volumen*. We are truly at the dawn of a new age of humanity."[5]

The new culture of hypermedia has given rise to even more interaction between text and image. The ease with which we can now manipulate images, combine them with text, and reproduce them instantaneously is changing the old order of readability, forcing us to rethink the concept of textuality. The literary text, if it is to have a future, will no longer be able to evade these new challenges.

21

The Rise of the Visual

The spectacle presents itself as an enormous unutterable and inaccessible actuality. It says nothing more than 'that which appears is good, that which is good appears.' The attitude which it demands in principle is this passive acceptance, which in fact it has already obtained by its manner of appearing without reply, by its monopoly of appearance.

—Guy Debord, *Society of the Spectacle*

According to Régis Debray,[1] our civilization has gone through three main eras: after the "logosphere"—the age of the *logos*—and the "graphosphere"— the age of the supremacy of writing—it has recently entered into a new age, the age of the eye, the "videosphere," which marks a sharp departure from the previous hierarchy of the senses. In antiquity, speech was considered the only effective way of communicating knowledge, and the ear was deemed more important than sight, capable of penetrating more deeply into the soul. Even a geographer like Strabo (first century) believed that sight was vastly inferior to the ear: "And he who claims that only those have knowledge who have actually seen abolishes the criterion of the sense of hearing, though this sense is much more important than sight for the purpose of science."[2] Similarly, Galen, a prominent physician of the second century, opposed the inclusion of illustrations of plants and flowers in his manuscripts.[3]

A new attitude toward images took hold in the richly decorated manuscripts of the Middle Ages. There seems to be no limit to the imagination of the illuminators in the creation of images—leaves, flowers, imaginary animals, angels and demons, or scenes from the Bible. The page is not only a text to be read but a space to be explored visually. In order to seduce their public, images had to inflame the imagination, amaze by their esthetic qualities, propose perplexing allegories, or evoke well-known religious narratives. The primary purpose of medieval illumination was to make reading attractive to a population that was largely illiterate; the richly decorated initials may be compared to gates through which the reader is enticed to enter into the text.

An important change occurred in the Renaissance, when scientists recognized the value of images for describing reality and their usefulness for experimental science. Within the space of a few years, Leonard Fuchs's *Historia stirpium* (1542), containing 512 very precise illustrations of plants, Conrad Gesner's *Historia animalium* (1551), with about a thousand illustrations, and Andreas Vesalius's *De humani corporis fabrica* (1543), whose illustrations were to remain authoritative for more than two centuries, were published. In the preface of his book, Fuchs expressly refuted Galen's position: "Who honestly would condemn images, which communicate information much more clearly than the words of even the most eloquent of men?"[4] It is clear that the authority of antiquity could no longer curb the use of images. With these books, the image gained legitimacy in the field of science for its incomparable descriptive and didactic value. Other kinds of images continued to be used, of course, for their emotional and allegorical value. Images were also used as tailpieces, to mark the end of a section of text.

Much later, a new use of images emerged in the representation of quantitative data in conjunction with time. A pioneer in this domain was Charles Joseph Minard, whose graph representing the losses of the Napoleonic army in the war with Russia is quite remarkable in its readability and its effectiveness.[5]

During the same period, visual resources began to be widely used in mass-circulation newspapers and magazines, thanks to the invention of a new process of printing, lithography (1796), and photography (1826). Even if images are still used to seduce and draw attention to the text, they are no longer mere illustrations but tend to become autonomous and to interact with the text in the production of meaning. At the same time, the field of documentary images is expanding rapidly. In the twentieth century, this new relationship between words and images will find its ideal medium in the magazine. Since the magazine page is designed to be perceived in the sweep of a gaze, the image has to create a kind of shock that will make the viewers hold their gaze long enough to awaken the desire to read. Since the sixties, this type of visual layout has spread to all kinds of subjects. Some publishers are even launching collections of books on abstract subjects aimed at an academic readership that use comic book techniques in which text plays only a secondary role.[6]

The juxtaposition of textual and visual elements on the page changes the economy of the text, which tends to leave descriptive and referential information to the images and focus on explaining the abstract elements or the connections between the data. It allows the readers to explore at their own pace, guided primarily by the illustrations. The new hybrid documents are much more difficult to paraphrase and may encourage the development of a kind of associative thinking in which the reader retains verbal and iconic elements in a personal synthesis strongly tinged with emotion that is based more on the effect felt than on the identification of a semantic macrostructure. Some critics believe that this could reintroduce a feature of oral culture into the culture of the Web, as does Derrick de Kerckhove, building on Ong's work.[7] Such a perspective, however, is unlikely, for it is difficult to imagine that our civilization would abandon the dominance of the eye to return to the oral culture of "hearsay." On the contrary, the computer will encourage the ever-increasing preeminence of the visual, exacerbating the dynamic tensions between oral and written language. In the past, this tension has been creative. According to Richard Lanham, it is at the root of our civilization: "From the contrast, the oscillation between the two kinds of culture, flows the power that has dynamized Western expression."[8]

The image may play on the emotional or the cognitive aspects of our brain. First, since images are interpreted by the limbic system, they seduce and speak directly to our emotions, producing an effect even before they are analyzed by the logical functions. The decoding speed of this system is less than two hundred-thousandths of a second, which is about how much time it takes an antelope to start running for its life when it glimpses a tiger's stripes in the grass of the savannah. When properly used, images have thus the power to create an emotional context of reception that will draw the reader into the text and affect the way we read it. We need only navigate on the Web and in hyperfictions to see that this use of the visual is becoming increasingly prominent. In many cases, the images aim to hold the uncertain and highly volatile attention of readers who are caught up in the pursuit of signs and must be seduced into devoting a moment of attention to a document.

Cognitively, the synthetic nature of images enables them to provide a global representation of a set of complex phenomena and to highlight relationships that would otherwise go unnoticed.[9] By presenting data on two or three axes, graphs can express visually relationships of causality, comparison, or opposition. Intertwined with a map, a timeframe, or both, a graph can thus replace significant quantities of text and give a better understanding of the phenomena. As an example, a map of Canada published in *The Walrus* (September 2005) uses a colored scale for representing variations in albedo—the percentage of reflected sunlight—on that country between 1984 and 2004, synthesizing 9.7 terabytes of data collected by 19 types of satellites that have photographed the country in more than 200,000 orbits. It is impossible to imagine that kind of information expressed in verbal language. Moreover, because of their spatial nature, images respond to contemporary readers' desire to go directly to what interests them, thus allowing greater control over the activity of reading.

As a universal converter of signs, the computer is not only good at producing graphs but can also translate any type of data into colored images or use new metaphors in order to express visually vast quantities of data: phylogenetic tree diagrams, time lines, peaks and valleys, river systems. Meta-search engines such as Grokker.com or Kartoo.com are trying to meet the new demands for visualization by presenting their search results graphically. This trend will certainly accelerate. Jay David Bolter goes as far as envisioning the possibility that "If hypertext calls into question the future of the printed book, digital graphics call into question the future of alphabetic writing itself."[10]

These two dimensions of images, the cognitive and the emotional, can certainly coexist, just as we have seen with the rhetorical aspects of language (see chapter 9, "Meaning and Effect"). They can even be perceived in a single glance because they call on different networks in our cortex. Thus, an illustrator can overdetermine a graph visually, giving it a shape that reflects the information provided—like a calligram, but with greater coherence, because its form and its substance are of the same nature. Readers who are used to the abundance of information provided by graphs will expect an author to use them whenever possible.

In creative texts, the digital poet often aims to combine fragments of text and iconic elements so as to create a textual work situated at the intersection of poem and image. This hybridization of text with the visual is characteristic not only of emerging literary production, but also of many information sites, in which the formatting of textual data draws extensively on the resources of graphic design. Because of the ease with which computers can process digital data, images are winning a legitimate place in communication. And in comparison to the tools available in oral language, their wealth is inexhaustible. Where poetic meter can only use variations in accent and duration, some forty phonemes, and a finite number of syllables, the visual realm offers text an incredible variety of size, color, shape, and arrangement, not to mention the richness of drawing, photography, and painting. As W. J. T. Mitchell observes, "Whatever the pictorial turn is, then, it should be clear that it is not a return to naïve mimesis, copy or correspondence theories of representation, or a renewed metaphysics of pictorial 'presence': it is rather a postlinguistic, postsemiotic rediscovery of the picture as a complex interplay between visuality, apparatus, institutions, discourse, bodies, and figurality. It is the realization that spectatorship (the look, the gaze, the glance, the practices of observation, surveillance, and visual pleasure) may be as deep a problem as various forms of reading (decipherment, decoding, interpretation, etc.) and that visual experience or 'visual literacy' might not be fully explicable on the model of textuality."[11] The innumerable means of seduction unleashed by the proliferation of images may also prove to be a challenge for a society. The image plunges viewers into the sensory world of perception, from which they often emerge imbued with a series of vague significations and connotations related to emotional effects that go beyond their society's univocal symbolic code and paralyze their critical thinking. This gives images a powerful fascination that may in some societies exacerbate tensions between modernity and age-old ways of living. The forging of a new alliance between words and images may be the biggest challenge of the education system in the years to come.

22

The Period, the Pause, and the Emoticon

The term *punctuation* designates a set of mechanisms in written language by means of which the author or publisher indicates the relationships among the various linguistic units of a text. It essentially covers phenomena involving segmentation into clauses and sentences. At a higher level, it also includes the division into paragraphs and chapters, as indicated by means of typographic devices known as "text punctuation," as opposed to "syntactic punctuation."[1]

Aristotle noted that punctuation was sometimes needed to allow readers to determine whether a particular word was related to the part of the sentence before it or after it. But punctuation marks began to appear with some regularity only in the third century BCE in Alexandria, with Aristarchus of Samothrace. In the first century CE, the Romans separated words with dots; later they adopted the *scriptura continua* of the Greeks, with no breaks between words.[2] There was no need to separate the words, since reading was essentially oral and was done by specialized slaves. St. Jerome introduced an innovation, however, in the fourth century, when he presented his translation of the Bible *per cola et commata*, with the text divided into meaningful sentences; these are the numbered verses still used today. By making it easier to quote or refer to the sacred texts, this contributed to making reading an activity under the control of the visual. But there was strong resistance from people who considered that the word of God could only be continuous.

The development of punctuation in the Middle Ages shows an increase in attention to the visual aspects of reading and to the facilitation of the reader's work by the addition of nonverbal clues to the text. This trend first appeared in Irish manuscripts of the seventh century, in which punctuation played an increasingly important role, becoming part of the decorative elements. This era also saw the introduction of quotation marks to cite excerpts from the Gospels. Later, various signs corresponding to more or less pronounced pauses were introduced, but there was no standardization. In the ninth century, the question mark appeared. In the twelfth century, certain scribes were still using only two signs, the comma and the dash (the equivalent of our period), while others used three to denote a minor pause, an internal major pause, and a final pause, respectively. It was only with the invention of printing and the works of the great Renaissance humanists such as Robert Estienne that the punctuation marks stabilized. In 1540 Étienne Dolet recognized six signs: "period with a tail" (comma), colon, period, question mark, exclamation mark, and parentheses. The semicolon came into use soon after, but without ever becoming absolutely necessary.

Of all these signs, it is undoubtedly the comma whose history reveals the most about the evolution of our relationship to text. Indeed, it raises the question of the overall system of reference a text should follow. Should it reproduce in writing the pauses that belong to diction and breathing or should it express logical relationships? The initial solution adopted was to give the comma the value of a pause in oral language, and it was also known as a "breath." In the seventeenth century, in French, for example, it was normal to place a comma between the subject and the verb in order to emphasize either of these words or to mark a pause by a person reading the sentence out loud (see chapter 6, "Standards of Readability"). This conception of the comma endured until very recently, and some grammar books still state that the comma indicates a brief pause. But this position is increasingly untenable, since the concept of a pause loses its meaning when reading aloud is no longer the normal way of reading. Today the eye does not need to see the mass of text in terms of segments to be spoken, but rather as clauses to be interpreted. As written language is seen as an autonomous semiotic system, the comma is becoming an indicator of purely logical segmentation, facilitating the division into semantic units. This position has only recently been taken into account in specialized books such as that of Jacques Drillon.[3]

In recent centuries, other signs have been proposed, such as the inverted question mark, which was suggested either to accompany a purely rhetorical question[4] or to indicate irony. But this sign was adopted only in Spanish, where it introduces an interrogative sentence; its function is thus primarily to facilitate oral reading by enabling the reader to adopt the appropriate intonation. The area where the number of signs has most increased recently is that of citation practices, in which variations in discourse are indicated by indentations, dashes, square brackets, italics, and ellipsis points, and, in commercial discourse, the signs for copyright and registered trademark. Quotation marks have also become so widely used that in recent decades they have even migrated to gesture and oral language.

But these signs are not sufficient, and there is no doubt that hypertext writing will invent its own system and its own punctuation marks. This is already true in the case of the color codes indicating the presence of a hyperlink, with one color used to show that a link is clickable and another to show that the link has been visited. There is also a trend toward the use of stylized drawings in e-mail messages to indicate different emotional states on the part of the sender: emoticons, or smileys. These pictograms combine various punctuation marks to express an iconic relationship with facial expressions, but they are not strictly speaking punctuation marks. In fact, while punctuation is still part of the verbal stream, since it provides instructions on how to divide that stream, emoticons belong to another code and represent a far-reaching attempt that transcends languages, an attempt to incorporate an iconic dimension into the written code. It is doubtful that the graft will take, because these signs encounter significant resistance based as much on the verbal roots of language as on the traditions surrounding written culture. Since they cannot be handled by the "shuttle" of comprehension, emoticons produce zones of nonmeaning in the textual machine, which are comparable to "failures" or, for those who know the code, interference in the verbal stream and recontextualization of the message; they function in the same way as a figure of speech that draws attention to itself. These pictograms obliquely and playfully reintroduce the subjective relationship of a person to his or her utterance, which also conflicts with the trend toward neutrality and objectivity in the traditional text. This double incompatibility will likely condemn them to remaining a marginal feature of writing, suitable mainly for e-mail and chat and for private relationships among adolescents, like their distinctive sociolinguistic codes.

23
Op. cit.

Like the high whine of the dentist's drill, the low rumble
of the footnote on the historian's page reassures: the
tedium it inflicts, like the pain inflicted by the drill, is not
random but directed, part of the cost that the benefits
of modern science and technology exact.

—Anthony Grafton, *The Footnote*

Scholarly books have had to develop various procedures for citing sources in order to avoid endlessly repeating the same information and wasting the reader's time. The oldest procedure is to give the complete reference in the first citation and after that to use only the Latin abbreviation op. cit. (for *opere citato*: in the work cited). This method is valid and effective as long as the reader reads closely and attentively, strictly following the thread of the text. But readers who approach a book selectively, using the index or the table of contents, will inevitably run into an "op. cit." that is not filed in their memory and will be obliged to go back ten or twenty pages or more to identify the work in question. In today's context of extensive reading, this venerable method of providing references imposes a linear process on the reader and results in an unjustifiable waste of time. A fossil remnant of oral discourse, this procedure is much closer to the culture of the *volumen* than to that of the codex. Its persistence in the scholarly community can be explained only by the inherent conservatism of activities related to high culture.

Fortunately, recent decades have witnessed the emergence of reference systems that are better suited to the tabularity of the book. One of the most efficient is the one established in 1951 by the powerful Modern Language Association (MLA),[1] which brings together scholars in language and literature. This system, which is used by the vast majority of North American publications in these fields, involves providing a list of works cited, organized in alphabetical order by author, at the end of the book, and simply following each citation with a reference to the author's name, the date of publication of the work in question (if there is more than one by the same author), and the page number. Thus, regardless of where readers open the book, they can in seconds precisely identify a source cited in the body of the text. This approach also has the advantage of enabling readers to take in the entire bibliography at a glance and assess how relevant or topical it is. In short, it gives readers greater control over their reading, making it easier and more efficient. The only disadvantage of this method is that it disrupts the apparent uniformity of the text with parentheses that are sometimes long and visually more cumbersome than just a superscript number. But this visual discontinuity is ultimately insignificant in comparison to the need to refer to a note that may sometimes be hard to find in order to ascertain the source of a citation. As long as the notes are only references, the reader can ignore them, and the continuity of the reading is not affected.

Scholarly books, however, as the heirs of the glossed manuscripts of the Middle Ages, have a profound affinity for content notes, whether as footnotes or as endnotes at the end of the chapter or the book. The function of this secondary discourse is to supplement the main discourse by presenting new hypotheses or comments on the work of other scholars. The notes may thus have a provocative quality that sometimes makes them the most interesting part of a work, and readers are often torn between wanting to read a note immediately and wanting to continue following the thread of the text despite the legitimate curiosity stimulated by the reference. This dilemma is well expressed by the historian Roger Chartier, for whom reading a footnote is "like having to answer the door when you're in the middle of lovemaking."[2]

These difficulties and hesitations of the book as it attempts to manage two texts simultaneously reveal its age-old predilection for the continuous thread, which was long considered the essential condition for the optimal functioning of the textual machine. We now see a trend toward the elimination of notes, as is suggested by the MLA model, or toward their "extermination," to use Pascal Quignard's term.[3] After all, it is up to the author to structure the text in such a way that readers can draw the most from it in the least time; notes should not be a way for authors to avoid their responsibility for organizing the text.

At the same time, the demands of tabularity suggest that readers should be able to easily locate the parts of a text that interest them and skip over digressions and irrelevant sections, in short, that they should not be tied to the continuous thread. This can be accomplished by the introduction of hierarchies and division into levels, or by placing secondary information that supplements the main text in separate blocks. The latter solution, which again recalls medieval glosses, is common in magazines and newspapers, whose large reading surfaces can easily accommodate juxtaposed blocks of text. Textbooks have also learned to draw on the possibilities offered by large formats. In contrast, most other books, with their smaller dimensions resulting mainly from the need for portability, do not have enough visual space to accommodate a complex layout. They have to prioritize the information and content themselves with making the reader move around between the main text and the scholarly notes, translations, or critical apparatus. The visual poverty of modern books is also justified by the greater readability afforded by a relatively narrow column of text; it is the result of a movement toward clean layouts that has only intensified over the centuries and that aims to neutralize interference and enable readers to concentrate on meaning. This modern position contrasts with the use of space in manuscripts and books in the early days of printing, when the main text was framed with glosses designed to maintain a constant relationship with it.

In a hypertext, there are no footnotes as such, but there are links to nodes of information that can be displayed in another place on the same page or in another window. Because of this, the medium has been compared, quite aptly, to a generalized system of footnotes, since all the entries are in principle placed on the same level, at least in the multisequential model, and they all refer to each other. Since there are no transitions between entries, every hyperlink confronts the reader with the same dilemma a reference number does: Is it worth the trouble of interrupting the thread of reading to consult this other entry, or can it be ignored? As we have seen, such questions can be resolved by the use of tabular hypertext and a larger screen surface.

24

The Reader

User or Consumer of Signs?

The mere fact of reading is itself a lulling
and semi-hypnotic experience.

—Marshall McLuhan, *From Cliché to Archetype*

We are sometimes reluctant to speak of "reading" with respect to hypermedia—and often in this book, I have employed the term *user* where one might
have expected the term *reader*. This is not only because of the affinities of
this new medium with spectacle, but also because of the particular way we
enter into relationship with it.

Reading consists in systematically collecting convergent clues belonging
to the same universe of meaning. In order for this gleaning to be successful,
at least two conditions must be met:

1. Readers must be able to manipulate the information as they wish:
   reread a passage, skip ahead, or go from the text to a table of contents
   or index.
2. They must be able to relate the signs presented to each other, using
   ordered operations that can essentially be shared with other people,
   so as to carry out most of the operations of meaning planned by the
   author, since the more of these they carry out, the more successful
   the reading will be. This, however, does not exclude the possibility that readers may also find in a text elements of meaning that the
   author did not intentionally produce but that come from the author's

unconscious or from the specialized filter used by the reader (see chapter 10, "Filters in Reading").

Reading as such hardly seems compatible with any other activity; it presupposes total attention on the part of the reader. We would therefore hesitate to describe consumers strolling through a shopping mall as readers, even though they may read the names of stores or labels on products. A reader is in essence someone who devotes a certain amount of time to perceiving, comprehending, and interpreting signs organized in the form of a message. In contrast, people engaged in zapping through hypermedia are like our shoppers, snatching bits of information on the fly—pitches, attempts at seduction by myriads of images, sounds, and advertisements. The speed of circulation, constant distractions, and lack of concentration preclude reading in the fullest sense. The same could be said about readers of hypertext, who are often doing something other than reading; they are looking at icons, selecting buttons, scrolling through columns of text, and so on. At times readers, at times spectators, at times just users: Such is the changing position of those who venture into vast hypertexts such as the Web.

As we have seen, it is possible to do a reading of a building and to consider it as a pseudo-text. And it is true that for an architect, going systematically through the structure of a building such as the Palais du Louvre and identifying its features is a form of reading. A tourist who goes in to take a quick look at the *Mona Lisa,* however, is just a user of the museum: he or she uses the organization of the space to serve purposes completely different from those of a student of architecture.

This raises the question of why we read—what is the motivation for this behavior that is one of the first things children learn in school and that has for millennia been the very basis of education? Once children have learned to read, they often cannot stop themselves from reading: Everything they see is an opportunity to experience anew the magic of reading, and any text beckons to them and activates the mechanism of reading. For some people, reading may become a constant activity, an indispensable routine, even a drug or, as for Valéry Larbaud, "an unpunished vice."[1]

We thus cannot equate the written sign with any other sign, whether humanly created or natural, although we sometimes speak metaphorically of the "great book of nature." The fundamental difference between reading and other semiotic operations lies in the particular quality of the signs manipulated in reading, and in the promise of meaning it makes to the reader, a promise that is nowhere more explicit than in the printed text, with its regularity and the additional enticement of typography and illustrations.

Once the operation of reading has begun, it is taken over by the regular operation of the textual machine—a means of staving off boredom for the reader or sustaining the semiotic function of reading by putting it on automatic pilot. The quasi-mechanical production of meaning made possible by the perfectly readable text produces a kind of hypnotic pleasure, which is all the more pervasive when the intellectual operations required by the text are more routine. This is undoubtedly the reason for the frequent accusation of intellectual laziness made against voracious readers of "lightweight" texts. Hermann Hesse, for example, recounted how he rediscovered the pleasure of this kind of reading when he found some newspapers in a hotel room: "And once again, I understood why people like to read newspapers. Bewitched by the network of links of information, I understood the charm of being a mere spectator, free of all responsibility."[2] And he went on to inveigh against newspapers.

Similar criticisms have been made of television. And more recently, it has been claimed that the Internet is responsible for what psychologists have named "Internet addiction disorder," a psychological syndrome that emerged in the mid-nineties and is said mainly to affect adolescents, who spend entire nights surfing the Net and are incapable of focusing on any other activity. Living only to be "connected," they are said to present severe withdrawal symptoms when forced to return to the "normal" world for too long. In fact, a similar psychological disorder was diagnosed in our civilization in 1605, when reading certain types of books was supposed to cause a state of stupefaction and addiction. According to the diagnosis provided by Miguel de Cervantes, reading tales of chivalry caused Don Quixote to lose his mind: "él se enfrascó tanto en su lectura, que se le pasaban las noches leyendo de claro en claro, y los días de turbio en turbio; y así, del poco dormir y del mucho leer, se le secó el celebro de manera que vino a perder el juicio" [he so immersed himself in those romances that he spent whole days and nights over his books; and thus with little sleeping and much reading, his brains dried up to such a degree that he lost the use of his reason].[3] By making books commonplace and readily available, the invention of printing gave rise to a form of psychological dependency that had until then been unthinkable: the uncontrolled consumption of novels. This kind of addiction was already attested around 1550 by Pierre de Ronsard's verses "Now I would read old Homer in three days: Therefore, my Corydon, lock well the door."[4]

After Cervantes wrote his inspired chronicle of this "disorder," it appears that it became part of accepted practices, and the supposed victims have done quite well in the end. When an entire civilization suffers from the same ill, it ends up becoming the norm, or even a virtue. Vladimir Nabokov had read ten thousand books by the end of his adolescence and Jorge Luis

Borges dreamed of living in a "Library of Babel," but no one ever suggested they should be institutionalized. In any case, no contemporary psychologist would dare to diagnose an RAD (Reading Addiction Disorder).

Now, with the World Wide Web gaining ground over print, it is commonly seen as a potential source of disorder. The Internet addict is a person who would like to consume everything there is to read or see on the Net, someone who rejoices at the idea of being in virtual contact with millions of people, pursuing with every mouse click a vague desire for communication that is as old as humanity and that today, as never before, holds the promise of immediate gratification.

But the new medium does not necessarily facilitate reading. One of the major obstacles hypertext creates for the activity of reading is to be found in its effect of decontextualization, when this effect is not mediated by the text or by the reader's cognitive activity. Indeed, there can only be reading if the elements to be decoded are subjected to the test of comprehension. And, as we have seen before, to comprehend a piece of information implies that one can relate it to a context of reception so as to look at it in light of what is already known. The most important part of comprehension, and one that is crucial for successful reading, is the activation in the reader's working memory of the previous knowledge needed for the proper processing of the information presented. The richer the cognitive context, the stronger the possibilities for the production of meaning; but if context is lacking, these possibilities tend toward zero.

When readers turn a page in a codex, they know they will find the continuation of the text they are reading—and the cognitive processing they have just carried out on that text enables them to construct a mental context that prepares them to receive new information. In navigation through a hypertext, the situation is very different, and with each new mouse click, there is a risk of moving further away from the context that was first selected. The context must therefore repeatedly be reconstructed, recalling the ancient myth of the Danaides, who were condemned to draw water with a jug that was pierced at its base. Readers can choose to revisit the same pages in a circular fashion, making the production of meaning monotonous, or they can just skim the surface of the pages without trying to understand them, but then they are like travelers strolling through the streets of Tokyo without knowing Japanese: Signs beckon to them, but they look at them indifferently, as at a spectacle. Our Web surfers may navigate until their wrists ache, but they may not be cognitively processing the information they encounter. To borrow Marshall McLuhan's image, they get the "massage" of the medium, but the message remains opaque and meaningless for them.

25

Intensive and Extensive Reading, or the Rights of the Reader

The transformation of the act of reading that we are witnessing today has been under way for several centuries. The traditional model, which was still dominant in the first half of the eighteenth century, required readers to assimilate a book from cover to cover. Jean-Jacques Rousseau, a victim of this intensive model, which he pushed to the extreme, describes in his *Confessions* the anguish he suffered as a result of reading in his youth: "The false idea which I entertained of things caused me to believe that, in order to read a book with profit, it was necessary to possess all the preliminary knowledge which it presupposed. I had no suspicion that very frequently the author himself did not possess it, and that he extracted it from other books as he required it. Possessed by this foolish idea, I was detained every moment, and obliged to run incessantly from one book to another: sometimes, before I had reached the tenth page of the work I wanted to study, I should have been obliged to exhaust the contents of whole libraries."[1] This did not prevent him from giving his character Julie in *The New Heloise* a similar precept: "To read little, and reflect much on our readings, or what amounts to the same thing, to talk a lot about them between us, is the way to digest them well."[2] This metaphor associating the book with food, and reading with the process of digestion and rumination, is one that, as Michel de Certeau has shown, was also strongly favored by mystics.[3]

This intensive mode of reading, which is characteristic of traditional culture, gave way to an extensive mode in the second half of the eighteenth century, a period that, according to Rolf Engelsing,[4] witnessed a revolution in reading. The growth of lending libraries and the proliferation of printed matter encouraged silent, rapid reading, with the emphasis on quantity rather than completeness or depth. The publication of Diderot and d'Alembert's *Encyclopédie* was emblematic of this new relationship to reading. There was, however, a reaction against it in the following century, which Gustave Flaubert referred to in his *Dictionary of Accepted Ideas* [*Dictionnaire des idées reçues*]: "Encyclopédie. Laugh at it pityingly for being quaint and old-fashioned; even so: thunder against it."[5] "Dictionary. Say of it: 'It's only for ignoramuses!' A rhyming dictionary?—For shame!"[6] The triumph of the novel in the same period may be seen as a swing back to the more intensive mode of reading, in which, as Roger Chartier stated, "the novel grabs hold of readers and controls them as religious texts once did."[7]

Nevertheless, the extensive model is largely dominant today, although it should be recognized that intensive reading and extensive reading can always coexist for an individual, in accordance with the objectives pursued and the nature of the texts read. With the tabularization of text, readers have been able to develop skimming strategies that are suited to their needs and that take full advantage of the speed of visual perception. This trend has been strengthened by the increasing desire of readers for as much control as possible over their reading and for the ability to move through texts as they please without being slowed down by artificial barriers due to the nature of the medium. In short, the reader has gradually stopped being a negligible factor, the necessary anonymous partner in written production, and has become a free agent who must be reckoned with.

The rise of the reader has reached an unprecedented level in recent decades and is reflected in the evolution of literary theory. As early as 1948, in a much cited text, Jean-Paul Sartre asked, "For Whom Does One Write?"[8] In 1957 Josep Maria Castellet published *La hora del lector* [*The Time of the Reader*]. A few years later, the debate between Roland Barthes and Raymond Picard over Barthes's *On Racine* legitimized the place of theory, and indirectly that of the reader, in interpretation. What was at stake in this debate was the possibility of making a personal reading of a work, examining it through the prism of a key idea or a particular theory. This operation has acquired greater legitimacy insofar as the text, in moving from the domain of the ear to that of the eye, has changed its instance of utterance to become an abstract, impersonal entity that can be detached from its author and its historical anchoring and offered for individual consumption and deconstruction in all its forms. Recognizing this as a new approach to the literary work, the reception theories of the Constance School established the reader as the horizon of reference for literary works. As Wolfgang Iser states: "It is evident that no theory concerned with literary texts can make much headway without bringing in the reader, who now appears to have been promoted to the new frame of reference whenever the semantic and pragmatic potential of the text comes under scrutiny."[9]

This new status of the reader also corresponds to a fragmentation of generally accepted reading practices, or indeed their dissolution, which is sometimes even forcefully demanded by the current culture. Thus, for Hans Magnus Enzensberger, "the reader is always right. . . . [He has] the right to leaf back and forward, to skip whole passages, to read sentences against the grain, to misunderstand them, to reshape them, to spin sentences out and embroider them with every possible association, to draw conclusions from the text of which the text knows nothing, to be annoyed at it, to be happy because of it, to forget it, to plagiarize it and to throw the book in which it is printed into the corner any time he likes."[10]

Even in schools, where it still managed to survive, the intensive model finally came under direct attack from within the system with the publication of Daniel Pennac's bill of "inviolable rights of the reader." In his bestseller *Comme un roman* [*Reads like a Novel*], whose success indicated a broad social consensus on the issue, the narrator persuasively enumerates the rights schools and adults should recognize for young people with regard to reading:

1. The right not to read
2. The right to skip pages
3. The right to not finish a book
4. The right to reread
5. The right to read anything
6. The right to "bovarysme" (a textually transmissible disease)
7. The right to read anywhere
8. The right to browse
9. The right to read out loud
10. The right to remain silent[11]

Who can fail to recognize in this portrait the readers of newspapers, magazines, and throw-away novels that we have all become?

Intensive, close reading, in which readers are guided by their activity and allow the text to lead them cognitively, has obviously not disappeared; it is still practiced with essays and literary texts in general. But we are witnessing a proliferation of situations of selective reading, in which readers move within a text according to their needs, skimming, selecting, and extracting only the elements that suit their purpose. The very nature of the Web will undoubtedly further accentuate this extensive mode of reading. Independently of the possible cost of Internet access, there are at least three reasons that favor reading with such urgency. First, reading on a computer screen does not allow readers to adopt as comfortable a posture as reading on paper, thus inducing them to read quickly and superficially rather than closely. Second, the texts being read are fragmented, and the many hyperlinks they contain tend to lead readers off in various directions, making them lose the initial context. Finally, the very poor interface of the texts and the rigidity of the hardware (keyboard, monitor) keep readers from being able to easily highlight or annotate passages that interest them or to consider texts read as candidates for rereading.

26

Metaphors for Reading

Although the verb *read* comes from the Anglo-Saxon *rædan*, "to explain," its French equivalent *lire* derives from the Latin *legere*, which means "to gather." Metaphorically, the operation of reading was thus associated with the action of gleaning a field. This conception of reading focuses on its process. But what is it that readers gather or collect? Of course, the activity of the reader varies according to the nature of the text. We scrutinize a contract to distinguish the layers of meaning designed to protect the signatories' interests; we devour a novel; we leaf through a magazine or newspaper.

The work of reading is often compared to the way bees collect pollen and turn it into honey. But the acquisition of knowledge through reading can take less peaceful forms. Thus, for Paul Valéry, reading is an action involving force, through which one extracts the substance of a book, leaving only a bloodless corpse: "A man of virtue (with respect to the mind) is in my opinion a man who has killed beneath him a million books, who in two hours' reading has drunk only the little strength that lay in that many pages. Reading is a military operation."[1]

With the digitization of written language and the availability of hundreds of billions of pages on the Web, the extensive mode of reading has already found new metaphors. Everyone today knows that you don't read hypermedia—you navigate or surf. Indeed, it is difficult to find a more apt way to describe the action of the cybernaut than as surfing on the crest of a constantly changing wave of information or navigating from node to node in an ocean of interconnected documents. Navigation here implies moving in an uncharted environment with no stable landmarks, no precisely plotted routes. It is an activity that also has perils and surprises, since one can easily get lost, find a new land, or be grounded on a reef (for many years, the dreaded "Error 404" was equivalent to this). Old addresses may disappear or move, and new ones appear; information is swept up in a constant and vast tidal movement. But can the intrepid navigator still be said to be reading? While he or she is obliged to read in order to get from one node to another, the reading will be discontinuous, quick, instrumental, and essentially oriented toward action. Like surfers, cybernauts often only glide on the froth of thousands of fragments of text. Rocked by the infinite tide of links and texts, they seem to aim primarily to bring back evidence of their navigation, often consisting of a few exotic sites.

With regard to writing, the navigation metaphor is much more ancient than its recent popularity might suggest. Ernst Robert Curtius tells us that Roman poets would compare writing a work to crossing a body of water on a boat. Virgil compared writing to casting off and setting sail; at the end of the work, the reader came into port.[2] Later, Dante cautioned his readers: "O ye, who in some pretty little boat, / Eager to listen, have been following / Behind my ship, that singing sails along, / Turn back to look again upon your shores; / Do not put out to sea."[3] There is another echo of this navigation metaphor in Céline: "The reader is not supposed to see the work. He is a passenger. He paid for his berth when he bought the book. He is not concerned about what happens on the bridge. He does not know how the ship is steered. He wants pleasure. Delectation. He has the book and wants to enjoy it, and that is what I apply myself to."[4] To Céline, Dante, and Virgil, it is up to the author to do most of the work of navigation; readers just follow, absorbed in pleasure, mere passengers on a boat whose captain is the author. On the Web, readers have become their own navigators, since there is no single text there and in order to move ahead, they have to constantly make decisions, following the nodes that appear on the horizon, which they glance over quickly without ever landing permanently.

It should be noted that the term *navigation* combines the concept of movement between documents with that of acquiring knowledge. Whereas in the civilization of the printed word, *leafing through* was considered secondary to *reading*, the opposite is the case for hypermedia, where the operation of reading is marginal to that of *surfing*. Hypermedia thus tends to give rise to a new way of consuming signs, situated halfway between the book and the spectacle, as was already mentioned in connection with hyperfiction. The action of surfing includes the movement of reading, which is based on the principle of the user deciding which hyperlinks to click on and how much time to devote to pages visited. But at the same time, the reader picks up little more than images or fragments of text. And without the movement provided by the text—especially in the narrative form—readers risk finding themselves going around in circles or getting bored. Thus this type of reading cannot satisfy the needs met by the traditional way of reading fiction.

Other metaphors have been suggested to describe the activity of reading. For Mark Heyer, "there are only three ways in which we gather information: by grazing, browsing, or hunting."[5] In *grazing*, readers systematically and conscientiously swallow everything offered them, like people watching television. In *browsing*, they go through a large amount of information without any specific objective in mind, as when leafing through a newspaper. *Hunting* involves seeking specific information.

Although these approaches can obviously coexist in a single person, they correspond to successive intellectual advances, the most recent of which, hunting, requires the most sophisticated tools. Readers looking for specific information already had complex instruments such as indexes, dictionaries, and encyclopedias. The computer allowed these operations to be further refined by making it possible, for example, to search for all occurrences of a particular word in a document. More recently, tools have even been developed that allow readers to find only the minimum of information, keeping unwanted elements masked. This approach is used, for example, by Web sites that provide adventure game players with hints in the form of specialized hypertexts designed to help those who are stuck on a particular puzzle and that provide just enough information for the player to go on, without spoiling the pleasure of discovery. If a player still does not see how to continue the game after receiving the first clue, he or she can ask for a second and then a third one, until the puzzle is completely solved. The most appropriate metaphor for this type of reading would be digging down through concentric layers or opening nested Russian dolls.

I shall redefine the grazing mode as continuous reading, which occurs when the reader aims to construct a significant whole out of a long text, even if the reading spans many sessions. This mode of immersive or sustained reading is most typical of the novel, in which users immerse themselves in order to create a fictional universe. It is also used, albeit with significant differences, with long essays where the reader seeks to master a series of arguments and concepts.

27

Representations of the Book

The book is culture in a concentrated form, and it has long been accorded a unique status as the repository of the word of God or the founding text of a society. Very early, the image of the codex held an important position in Christian iconography. In Ravenna, Italy, there are mosaics from the fifth century in which the book is held up as a talisman, and there are even little libraries of codices in the mausoleum of Galla Placidia. "The popular belief in a book in which God records each person's sins and virtues"[1] appears to date from this period. There are innumerable representations of Christ enthroned and of the evangelists Luke, John, and Matthew with open codices in their hands, as well as of Mark's lion holding a codex with a red cover in its paws. These same motifs are repeated endlessly in the sculptures that adorn the tympana of Romanesque churches. A symbol of the Revelation, knowledge, and truth, the book is the quintessential mythical object of Christianity. For centuries it was central in painting. In *The Virgin and Child with Saints Dominic and Thomas Aquinas*, by Fra Angelico, the saints are each holding an open codex for reading by the faithful or by onlookers. Even the Virgin was generally represented with a book in her hand—what better guarantee of piety and wisdom? In a painting by Simone Martini (fourteenth century), she is holding a partly open book while concentrating on the message the angel is delivering to her. In Leonardo da Vinci's *Annunciation* (fifteenth century), the book is presented even more imposingly, placed on an enormous lectern in front of the Virgin. In the *Madonna of the Magnificat*, by Sandro Botticelli (fifteenth century), the Madonna is writing the text of the Magnificat in an open codex. Luca Signorelli, in *The Holy Family* (fifteenth century), not only placed a book in the Virgin's hands; he also placed a second one open on the ground. Two more examples among a great many others are *Madonna of the Goldfinch*, by Raphael, and a Jan Van Eyck painting of the Virgin absorbed in reading, her eyes demurely cast down on the pages of the book.

During the period when, as a result of printing, the book was becoming a mass medium, its status as a cultural object was further strengthened. There were a large number of portraits in which the subject was depicted holding a book, including *Portrait of a Young Stranger*, by Andrea del Sarto, and portraits of boys or girls by Bronzino.

As Martine Poulain has shown, it is because the Bible was a symbol of faith that religious painting gave a special place to the book. In less devout times, the book was to become a symbol of knowledge, and libraries were used as scenery for the rich and powerful. In later centuries, the book continued to occupy a place in painting, but its importance was diminishing, even though, in the nineteenth century, there were images of readers in works by such painters as Pierre-Auguste Renoir, Edgar Degas, Édouard Manet, Maurice de Vlaminck, Vincent Van Gogh, and Paul Cézanne. In the twentieth century, the place of the book became even more limited. While women were shown reading in works by Henri Matisse, Pablo Picasso, Balthus, and Juan Gris, and the newspaper made its appearance in paintings, the book was no longer an attribute of knowledge or power. Books were still a major motif in still lifes, but they were depicted as old and tattered, as in the paintings of Pierre Skira (see, for example, *Nature morte aux livres* and *Vanité*). Its expulsion from the collective imagination had begun. The stage was set for the appearance of new media. A study of the environments in which interview subjects have been photographed in recent decades would show the increasingly prominent presence of a computer on a table or desk. Far from being an attribute of decision makers alone, the computer now tends to be part of the representation of any intellectual profession. The bookshelves in the background may still be a symbol of knowledge for academics or experts being questioned, particularly on subjects related to the law, but the computer guarantees the modernity of their views and their capacity to master complex fields, because it is now the computer, and no longer the book, that provides access to the totality of human knowledge.

28

The Role of the Publisher

While speech is essentially transitory, writing makes it possible to stabilize semantic configurations and give them a certain permanence in a particular medium. Texts engraved on stone were destined to survive for centuries, and it was impossible to make any corrections. This was still largely true for the manuscripts recopied by the monks in the *scriptoria* of the Middle Ages. But with the advent of electronic media, text has become eminently malleable. It can be erased in a fraction of a second and modified, transformed, or corrected effortlessly and indefinitely. The permanence of text is now a thing of the past.

Is the very concept of publishing doomed to vanish as well? Traditionally, publishing consisted of making available to the public a manuscript that an author had produced in the privacy of his or her study, within that exclusive and sometimes possessive relationship paper tends to create with the hand that writes. In submitting the manuscript to a publisher, the author entrusts the publisher with the task of conveying a symbolic production into the realm of commercial exchange. This involves the publisher taking charge of the standardization of the text, the typography, the layout, the choice of format and paper, the graphic design, the printing, and the distribution. These various functions, which require the services of many experts, transform the manuscript into a social object fit to enter the circuit of consumption and find its readership. The paratext, a kind of discourse around the work, provides an interface between the work and its readers, who will be attracted to the work because of their reading expectations resulting from its belonging to a particular genre, as indicated by the cover and other clues and enticements such as the title, the summary, the author's introduction, the illustrations, and the layout. In comparison with the initial manuscript, the book therefore has considerable added value.

All these barriers are telescoped in an electronic text, which can be made accessible on the Internet in a matter of hours once its author considers it finished. Often an author will even post a text before it is really finished, in order to elicit comments from the first readers and polish the work. There is thus no longer any obligatory filter between the producer of the text and its readers, and practically no gap in time. This has consequences for the nature of the text itself: Knowing that they can constantly rework their texts, authors may take less care in polishing them. For this reason, publishers will still be necessary, especially in an information-based society, first of all because specialized work with high added value is needed to arrange texts in standardized, consistent formats that facilitate reading. Above all, a publishing structure, by creating collections for specific readerships and approaches, carries out the necessary task of filtering publications for well-defined interpretive communities, to whom it provides an implicit guarantee that the texts offered are worthy of their interest.

29

The CD-ROM and Nostalgia
for the Papyrus Scroll

Optical discs have huge capacities for storing information, the limits of which we have hardly glimpsed, even with DVDs. When the first CD-ROMs arrived on the market in 1985, Microsoft organized a major conference on the potential impact of a medium that could provide instant access to what at the time were considered colossal quantities of data. It is interesting that the collection of papers from the conference, which was edited by Steve Lambert and Suzanne Ropiequet, bore the title *CD-ROM: The New Papyrus*, thus placing the new technology of the text in the realm of the papyrus, of which it is the worthy heir. One might see in this title a desire to legitimize electronic publishing on CD-ROM in the eyes of intellectuals by connecting it to the long tradition of the book, whose existence began with the papyrus. Yet I cannot help thinking that this metaphor expressed the feeling that there was a definite kinship between the *volumen* and the way the book is conceived in hypertext.

As we have seen, the papyrus scroll provides no markers to facilitate the reader's task. Designed to be unrolled from left to right, it can be read only by going through its columns of text from beginning to end. Readers are thus supposed to follow the thread of the text just as they would follow the thread of a speech or a conversation. Unlike the modern book, which since the emergence of the codex has seen the gradual creation of a large number of markers based on the tabularity of the text, the papyrus provides few clues that allow readers to manage their reading activity effectively. Contemporary readers suddenly confronted with a familiar book in the form of papyrus scrolls would not recognize it. They would have trouble finding a specific section of the text, since there would be no table of contents; locating a particular chapter, since there would be no running heads; finding a particular quotation, since there would be no page numbers; locating references to a specific author, since there would be no index; or determining the sources used in a scholarly work, since there would be no bibliography. And it would not be easy for readers to find where they had left off reading, since there would be no paragraphs or page numbers.

Should we do away with millennia of progress in the technology of printed matter and make the new medium as opaque as the ancient papyrus scroll, on the pretext that hypertext owes nothing to the book and ought not to imitate its structure? Is the future of text to be found in the past? Opacity in navigation may be justified in the case of hyperfictions and mysteries, but the on-screen reading of Web pages in plain html is very similar to the kind of reading imposed by the papyrus: In both cases, readers follow a column of text. It should be noted, however, that modern text processing offers more and more tabular tools, which make it possible, for example, to display text in the form of whole pages or even double pages, to go directly to a given page, or to move through a text by following notes, illustrations, or comments. The Acrobat Reader program is even more sophisticated, particularly in its search function, and can display the table of contents of a document or show miniature previews of the pages opposite the text column, allowing the user to move around in the text by clicking on these elements.

Readers in the ancient library of Alexandria probably did not suffer because of the limitations of the papyrus scroll; these became noticeable only by comparison with the tabular markers introduced with the codex. But once the limitations of an old way become apparent, there is no turning back. While the computer is changing our reading habits today, this does not mean we have to go back to the outmoded technology of the papyrus. Rather, we should seek ways to use the machine to give readers even greater control over their activity than that afforded by the codex. The screen can win readers over in the long term only if it builds on the achievements of print culture while at the same time freeing itself from the limitations inherent to that medium.

30

Giving the Reader Control

One of the radically new variables hypertext technology has introduced into reading is the ability of the author to control the reader's path through a body of text. Up to now, this power was exclusive to oral discourse. Everyone has experienced a situation in which a person is able, before consenting to speak or continue speaking, to impose specific behavior on his or her listeners: silence, the respectful display of all the outward signs of attentive listening, or even a particular posture. Since oral exchange belongs to the realm of presence, it gives speakers an authority proportional to their physical or institutional power. It should be no surprise, then, that in many languages, hearing is equivalent to understanding, hearing being the capacity to mentally process data strung together and communicated through speech.

As explained above, the advent of written language disrupted this age-old association, putting comprehension under the control of the eye. Writing, much better than oral language, is able to crystallize a sequence of thoughts into the elements required for a reader to be able to recreate it. Once fixed in writing on a clay tablet or a page, verbal information is no longer necessarily sequential. It has left the temporal realm and entered that of space, escaping from its author to belong to the mind that grasps it. This occurs through visual perception, and the eye can as readily scan, gaze, scrutinize, follow a line of text, select another line, or backtrack. Indeed, the analytical power of the eye serves as both an entry point and a metaphor for the activity of analysis. It is the eye of the master that records everything, equally capable of instantly taking in broad perspectives as of focusing on a single detail. The visibility of the text is all the greater for being displayed on the double page of the codex.

The advent of hypertext has made this ancient split between eye and ear rather problematic. In hypertext, written language is no longer governed by surface relationships, but by deep internal relationships. Since just one screen page can hide all the rest, authors are able to completely control their readers' path and their exposure to the message by revealing only certain layers of the text according to the order and pace of their choices, like ancient storytellers before the assembled tribe—or like that master of suspense, Alfred Hitchcock, who wanted to prohibit latecomers from entering showings of his films. The figure of the master, which has never disappeared from teaching, can now accompany the interactive textbook. This opens up enormous possibilities for education. Thanks to computer technology, authors can exert a degree of control over readers that they lost when they abandoned oral language for writing. In some cases, then, hypertext represents a fundamental break with the division that has existed between oral and written language, and marks a return to an archaic situation.

The implications of this situation are not always fully appreciated by theorists, many of whom have seen fit to discuss only hypertext's positive aspect, that of freeing readers from the linearity of the book. Yet one need only examine the possibilities of hypertext to discover the many ways it can subordinate the reader to the will of the author. For example, hypertext can be used to impose the pace of reading by having the text scroll continuously in a window so small that it only shows one or two lines at a time. This is the worst possible subjugation of the reader—indeed, a person watching a text scroll down the screen without being able to stop the movement is no longer a reader, but a spectator or a listener. Of course, film has accustomed us to something similar with the rolling of the credits or the presentation of a summary to provide context at the beginning of a movie. Seeing whole lines disappear at the top of the screen before there is time to decipher them is not a pleasant situation for a reader, but it is not particularly frustrating for someone viewing a spectacle. After all, we expect to be dazzled by a spectacle, and not necessarily to understand or retain everything. The same is true in a listening situation when we miss words because of ambient noise or poor transmission. Listeners who are not in a position to have a word or a sentence repeated have to make do with what they have been able to grasp. The situation is completely different in reading, where in principle the message should be entirely under the reader's control.

Hypertext can also be used to force readers to cover the elements of a work in a predetermined order—even if that order is random. This potential for control opens new horizons for training manuals and textbooks. It also offers new creative possibilities. For example, hypermedia fiction such as *Myst* and *Riven* involve the reader navigating in an environment that has no reference points and is as indecipherable as possible; it would be counterproductive to allow the reader to move around transparently at will.

By moving writing from the two-dimensional space of the page to three-dimensional space, hypertext also changes the nature of text. Since the eye can no longer take in all its components as easily, the metaphor of the fabric of the text will have to be reexamined. But how can we deal with depth without loss of transparency? The new potential for control by the reader will no doubt make it desirable to establish a bill of rights for hypertext users, like the one Daniel Pennac proposed for readers of the novel (see chapter 25, "Intensive and Extensive Reading"), which represented a departure from the authoritarian model of intensive reading. For the hypertext user, these rights should be as follows:

1. The right to know at the outset at least the approximate volume of text provided as well as the number of images and the total duration of sound and video clips
2. The right to enter the text at any point
3. The right to read the units on a single subject one after the other
4. The right to easily find and reread a passage read previously
5. The right to annotate pages read

In actual fact, there is no need for such a bill of rights to be enacted, as it will eventually come about of itself. A text can attract readers and hold their attention only insofar as they feel respected. A reader who is not satisfied by a work will soon abandon it. Thus, instead of turning away from the codex, designers of hypertext would be well advised to incorporate the tabular characteristics that have for centuries made it an indispensable aid to learning and intellectual curiosity.

This being said, it is likely that the habit of writing for this new medium will lead to changes in textuality that are as significant as those resulting from the shift from the *volumen* to the codex. It is impossible to foresee all these changes. But readers are unlikely to give up the power to manipulate texts and adapt them to their needs. The more control they can exercise over their activity through the configuration and ergonomics of objects on the screen, the more effective and enjoyable it will be. I will not elaborate on the purely material control of the appearance of objects; it is obviously satisfying for readers to be able to choose the background color and font size according to their preferences or their vision problems. Similarly, the ability to change the dimensions of windows and the arrangement of objects helps provide the comfort needed for sustained reading. Informational texts should also be designed to give readers the maximum of tabular controls. In principle, electronic documents should provide all the elements available to readers of books—and something more. Readers clearly should be able to choose when they will go on to another paragraph or another page—insofar as the concept of page is still applicable to hypertext. This first type of control, which is purely physical, involves the ability to read a text at one's own pace.

At a higher level, readers should be able to have an overall view of the work. They should be able to situate the segment they are reading and visually grasp its function in the overall organization of the work. For museum collections, tabular clues may include lists by theme, author, or time period. For example, readers who enter the database of a museum should be able to get an overview in the form of a list of titles or a series of thumbnails. They should certainly not be limited to seeing only works whose titles they enter in a search field; such a model would exclude anyone who did not know beforehand what was in the database. Nor should users be forced to navigate without landmarks; invoking "the spirit of discovery" inherent in hypertext technology to keep users in the dark infantilizes them by denying them access to information they need in order to manage their reading and the time they devote to it. They can be provided with a map of the building in which they are circulating or a plan of the site. There can also be a list of what they have viewed in comparison with what remains to be viewed, or a graph showing the node where they are in relation to its immediate surroundings.

In short, the computer screen should visually communicate a great deal of information that in the physical world is provided by the spatial dimensions of places visited, or in the world of the book by peripheral tactile or visual sensations such as the thickness of the volume. Similarly, bookmarks should be placeable at various points and seen at a glance, as with a book. It should be possible to move quickly from one place to another and to go back and forth between them and to make annotations that can be found and reread, corrected, or expanded during the next visit.

While it must be recognized that a standard screen is still a long way from the kind of workspace provided by a table, there is clearly a trend toward an increase in the surface area of the screen. When screens have more resolution and double or triple the surface area that was till recently still considered normal, the computer will no doubt offer a very pleasant environment and the screen will look more and more like a "natural" space in which to carry out operations of reading and writing.

31
Text and Interactivity

Hypertext differs radically from the book in that it can respond to the movements of the user. This is a major advantage for an electronic textbook, since the screen can be the equivalent of the board in front of the classroom, and students can use it to play demonstration or animation sequences as many times as needed. The software can also mask key words in order to stimulate readers' curiosity and hold their attention; to reveal these words, users just need to hover over them with the mouse. This is an elementary form of interactivity, which may be defined as the capacity for users to create events on the page. To hold users' attention, every page of a hypertextbook should include an operation carried out by them: making a window appear, uncovering a correct answer, changing the color of a sentence by correcting it, putting an incorrect element in the trash, showing relationships between items of information, running an animation sequence or demonstration, and so on.

In the case of text on paper, the activity of reading is associated with specific physical characteristics that are generally perceived subliminally: the thickness and other characteristics of the paper, the smell of the ink and binding, and so on. A book can be touched, held in the hands, and felt as a real presence. In comparison, a text on the screen is grasped purely through sight and may remain a cold abstraction for readers. It is therefore important to provide every means possible to enable readers to experience the screen as a warm presence capable of responding to their impulses.

Interaction using the mouse is obviously a way of involving the reader's body. Reading is thus associated with muscle action. The use of icons is another way to break with the abstraction of printed matter. Images encourage a different mode of reading, a symbolic reading that weaves a subtle emotional relationship with the text. Color is perceived by peripheral vision, and its use gives the text a warmer, more alive dimension, which compensates for the poor definition of the screen and adds to the richness of the visual material. Used consistently, it helps readers orient themselves in the screen environment.

The computer can also add virtual events in order to translate certain visual or auditory aspects of the experience of reading a physical book. For example, the sound of a page turning can recreate in readers-spectators the impression of reading a book printed on heavy paper or an ancient parchment—a sound effect that is already common in electronic encyclopedias and games such as *Riven*. The turning of pages may also be accompanied by optical effects analogous to those that have long been used in film: fade to black, dissolve, spiral dissolve, puzzle effect, and the rest. The time it takes for these operations has an important effect on reading; when fast, they push the reader to advance quickly, and when slow, they impose a measured pace and a more attentive approach to the content of the page.[1]

32

Managing Hyperlinks

The normal mode of navigation in a hypertext is by clicking on links that provide access to information nodes on the same page or another page: texts, images, and visual or sound clips. At first glance, this operation is simple and obvious. However, clicking on a word in a text is always a leap into the unknown, since it involves leaving an established context. And the reader does not always know to what extent the new data found will match the previous context. Perhaps the new node will present only an association that is quite distant from the subject at hand, one the reader could very well have done without. Perhaps it will branch off in a new direction, forcing the reader to provide a new context and suspend the reading configuration already established. And the reader-navigator cannot predict the scope of further developments—whether the link followed will lead to a brief excursion, a long detour, or even a radical departure from the textual thread being followed. Therefore it would be no exaggeration to say that the problem of links is the "weak link" in the new textual organization represented by hypertext.

A partial solution to these problems of decontextualization would be to give readers a way of knowing immediately what type of content each of the links on a page will lead to. Ideally, it should be possible to distinguish between endosemic links, which develop a concept in greater detail, and exosemic links, which are related to the hyperlinked word only by association. With the possibilities opened up by XML, it would also be possible to distinguish between links pointing to different types of information such as bibliographic references, definitions, or supplementary explanations.

Some people have recommended not making links on single words, but only on phrases. A phrase can restrict meaning more than a single word and thus provides a context that allows readers to have a clearer idea of what they are clicking on. This solution, however, also has the effect of substantially increasing the space occupied by colored links on the page, making them more blatant and intrusive.

33

I Click, Therefore I Read

In a physical book, all the pages are present, but in the case of hypertext, they appear only at the request of the user. This creates a particular kind of reading situation, the main characteristic of which is that readers have to constantly make choices by clicking on one button or another to make various units of information appear. Each button, each hyperlink, is thus an invitation to move forward, a promise of content. Through this intrinsic mechanism of revelation, this system relies essentially on child psychology. Anticipating what is today known as the "law of the hammer" (namely, that a child who discovers a hammer will try to hammer everything available), Paul Valéry observed how children respond to things in their environment, wanting to pull every ring they encounter, open every door, turn every crank, climb every staircase.[1]

Movement by means of mouse clicks gives readers a sense of control—insofar as the program allows them such control, of course—and a feeling of being able to give free rein to their impulses. The mouse is the exact equivalent of the remote control for television, whose capacity to change channels with a mere touch has modified the habits of television viewers, encouraging the sometimes frenetic consumption of snatches of programs. Similarly, navigation by means of a mouse tends to give rise to chaotic, extremely rapid movement that is not very favorable to reading. The reading of hypertext is thus marked by immediacy and urgency. Excited by the promise of revelation implicit in hyperlinks, readers want to reach their destination before even beginning to read. This way of reading is very far from the meditative or intensive reading valued in the past. In fact, these two approaches call on very different cognitive operations, which may be associated with the fundamental mechanisms of assimilation and accommodation described by the psychologist Jean Piaget. In the former, the subject incorporates objects perceived by creating the appropriate schemata as necessary; in the latter, the subject only temporarily adapts [existing] schemata to new objects in order to experience the difference in relation to what he or she already knows. The latter mode is that of a perpetually unsatisfied, superficial curiosity. As French sociologist Gilles Lipovetsky shows with regard to television, readers who are "zappers" do not expect their activity to bring them any knowledge or, even less, to change their lives; all they want is to stave off boredom: "In fact, zappers are always on the lookout for a program that will hold their attention, but without wanting to make any effort: They want to be instantaneously drawn in. They are bored by the programs, but cannot tear themselves away from the screen. There is something tragic in the condition of the zapper, the tragedy of the television viewer's desire that can never be truly fulfilled."[2] Zapping, whether in relation to TV or to the Web, corresponds to a constant need for the renewal of cognitive operations; it recreates in the visual or written realm the sudden changes of subject found in oral conversation. In this sense, it is fundamentally opposed to the very purpose that has guided traditional writing, which is to develop a subject exhaustively in order to provide a new synthesis. For a whole series of reasons due to the still immature state of the medium—the current eyestraining backlit monitors, all of which hinder comfortable reading; the cost of access to the network; absence of proper publishing protocols—the dynamics of the Web are transforming reading into a frenetic activity in which readers are constantly on the surface of the self, surfing over the waves of the meanings offered, carried away by a kaleidoscope of images and fragments of text that are forgotten as soon as they are perceived. According to Régis Debray, "the exhilaration of the zapper commanding a push-button world is a throwback to a primitive state of intoxication."[3] Without desire carrying it forward and without the mechanisms that would enable conscious and thoughtful activity, this form of reading is condemned to flit about in repetition, with the zapping speeding up in direct proportion to the boredom generated.

Navigation on the Web thus cannot be that self-hypnosis that readers of novels let themselves be lulled into, floating on a language and an imaginary for hours, sometimes weeks on end. Don Quixote, that "long, thin graphism,"[4] would probably not have lost his mind if he had had to click his way through the novels of chivalry he read: "If you want the knight to rescue his lady-love, click on this word. Click here if you want him to continue on his way." This need to click to obtain text could easily put modern navigators off reading.

This raises questions about the desire that impels the reader forward. Readers starting a book are constantly carried beyond what they are reading by the promise of an essential revelation—whether this be the dénouement of the plot of a novel, an appreciation of the mystery of a life, or a broader comprehension of society.

Perhaps the desire to read is at its most paradoxical when it takes us outside the text. As we have seen, books do not hold our attention in the same way as spectacle, since readers can always stop reading to explore possible points of contact between their networks of associations and the text. Similarly, they are always at liberty to backtrack to reread a passage and reflect on it. Reading is thus ideally suited to the work of cognitive sedimentation; it makes it possible to inscribe an utterance in time, giving it volume and density, while in the world of primary orality, it is possible to approach density only through repetition.

But of course, for this enrichment of the mind to occur through reading, readers have to be receptive, and not just reading out of a sense of duty or in a purely mechanical way. Andre Gide describes this in a passage in his *Journals*: "I am reading Carlyle, who annoys me and awakens my enthusiasm at one and the same time. I made the mistake of reading the second lecture (of *Heroes and Hero-Worship*) out of a sense of duty. I never penetrated it. This is absurd. I should never read anything in that way. The first lecture, on the other hand, made such an impression on me that I thought I should never finish reading it. Every line called for a quarter of an hour of reflexions and musings."[5]

When the mind is open to what it is reading, information gathered from the text is fully related to the sum of previous knowledge, which enables the assimilation of the new thought and the construction of fresh meaning. Michel de Certeau spoke of this as "poaching"; moving through a book like a poacher hunting, the reader is always on the lookout for game to nourish thought.[6] Roland Barthes describes the paradox of the temptation to leave off our reading at exactly the moment when it interests us the most: "I would say, precisely because I always place myself on the plane of sensitivity and pleasure, I don't read much, either because the book bores me and then I drop it, or because it excites me, it pleases me, and then I always want to look up from it and continue thinking or reflecting on my own. Which makes me quite a bad reader in quantitative terms."[7] Meandering and a state of floating attention were Michel de Montaigne's preferred mode: "There I turn over now one book, and then another, on various subjects, without method or design. One while I meditate, another I record and dictate, as I walk to and fro, such whimsies as these I present to you here."[8]

34

The End of the Page?

The student of literature and philosophy is prone to be
concerned with book "content" and to ignore its form.
This failure is peculiar to phonetic literacy in which the
visual code always has the "content" that is the speech
recreated by the person engaged in reading.

—Marshall McLuhan, *The Gutenberg Galaxy*

Form and content have sometimes been closely interdependent. The scribes
of Sumer used round tablets for texts on the economy, square tablets for
literary texts, and tablets in the shape of a liver for divinatory texts.[1] In the
papyrus scroll, the word *pagina* designated a column of text measuring on
average eight to twelve centimeters in width, with about thirty characters per
line. Remarkably, newspaper and magazine columns today have these same
dimensions. This means that these dimensions are not due to mere cultural
habit, but are based on the physiology of the eye. Experimental studies have
in fact shown that, during reading, the eye moves forward not in a linear
fashion, but rather by jumping from one point to another, fixing very briefly
on each one. The longer a line, the more erratic the movement of the eye will
be, hindering reading by veering from the line being read to the one above or
below. This affinity of the eye for a short line is the basis of the current page
format, with a line of text rarely exceeding seventy characters.

   With the adoption of the codex, the term *pagina* very soon came to correspond to our current concept of the page. It was the folding of the folio in two

and then in four that led to the appearance of the "modern" page, consisting of one side of a double page. There is nothing self-evident about this form: Chinese books were printed on one side of the paper only and folded in a fan. The page retains the column's taller-than-wide shape, which gives the text stable boundaries that facilitate the quantification of information and the use of references (see chapter 8, "Toward the Tabular Text"). Far from being gratuitous, the use of regular margins has semantic effects, and it influences how the text is read, often without the reader being aware of it.[2]

Because of the advantages of this traditional interface for the reading of text, a virtual equivalent of the codex page could well be essential for sustained reading on the screen and for the smooth migration of the universal library to the new space of culture. But there is nothing obvious about the transposition of the page to the computer. Almost fifteen years have gone by since the birth of the Web, and yet the virtual page is still in its infancy.

It should be noted that the first computers had no screens and communicated their results on rolls of perforated paper. The first screens made their appearance toward the end of the fifties and quite naturally borrowed their shape from television. It took several years before anyone thought of using the term *page* to designate what was displayed on the screen and before a consensus was reached on the use of this term. In the computer world, the term *stack* was first used to designate a memory space, and later, *card* or *hypercard,* the latter being the name of a 1987 hypertext writing software for the Macintosh, which popularized the concept. Since the first texts were very short, they were also called nodes or paragraphs. Certain authors of hyperfiction, such as Moulthrop, use the term *space,* while Terence Harpold speaks of lexias, borrowing the term Roland Barthes used (*lexie*) for the units of analysis into which he divided "Sarrazine" in *S/Z.* Espen Aarseth speaks of the texton. Still others speak of the screen, or the screen page, to avoid confusion with the printed page.[3] But since the use of the Web has become widespread, it seems that the term *Web page,* or simply *page,* a word that for centuries designated the basic unit of written culture, has taken root in the digital world. Its adoption testifies to the often-observed fact that we naturally tend to understand new phenomena in terms of the familiar, even if it may be metaphorical.

The screen "page," however, does not really possess the characteristics of its counterpart in the print world. In a paper medium, the page is a material entity with fixed dimensions, containing a segment of text in which the number of characters is more or less constant within a single book. It is a space in which the text is lined up until the space is filled. As a purely material constraint, the printed page only loosely corresponds to a unit of semantic content: a unit of meaning such as a paragraph—which is very important for managing the reading process—may go on for several pages, or conversely, many units of meaning may coexist on a single page. Only a major semantic break, indicated by means of a new chapter or section, justifies starting a new page. The foregoing needs to be qualified, however, in the case of magazines, where the thematic unit increasingly coincides with the page. It should also be noted that magazine articles usually begin on a left-hand page, while in books, the right-hand page is normally reserved for the beginning of a chapter. As the typographer Fernand Baudin observes, "as long as there have been scribes and typographers, the visual unit in the space of the book has been the double page."[4] Thus, on paper, it is not the page, but the double page, that must be considered, and its economy varies according to the purpose of the text and the cultural conventions governing the medium.

The main characteristic of the screen page, and one that distinguishes it from the codex, is that it is not limited to fixed dimensions, since the main window can have vertical and horizontal scroll arrows. Publishers of online texts therefore need to use completely new markers for textual material. At least three major questions have to be considered. The first is to determine the amount of information on a basic page, which I will call the *mass of the page*. Research done in the eighties suggested that it was advisable to limit the length of the textual unit to one idea or one learning element. *Hypertext Hands-On*,[5] published both in print format and in hypertext, came to the conclusion that a paragraph that seemed to be the right length on the paper page was much too long for reading on the screen. Conversely, a unit of text that seems to be a satisfactory length on the screen appears terse and insufficiently developed on paper. But it does not seem possible to formulate general rules for the whole area of digital writing, in which different types of texts call for different modes of reading and organization.

As soon as the text mass exceeds the dimensions of a single screen, the author has to choose the dominant metaphor for the mode of reading: moving from page to page horizontally, as in the codex, or scrolling vertically, as in the medieval *rotulus*, which was unrolled from top to bottom for public proclamations. There are no simple, obvious solutions, as has been noted by all those who have published texts of any size on the Web, such as Jerome McGann's *Rossetti Archive*, Michael Groden's *James Joyce's* Ulysses *in Hypermedia*, or Michael Best's *Internet Shakespeare Editions*.[6]

The advantage of the horizontal scroll window is that the text is displayed in a fixed window, whose content readers refresh by clicking on the "next page" arrow. This is the model that is naturally chosen for books that have already been printed and are being offered in e-book format or by Google Books. Displaying the text in a page of fixed length may, however, impose limitations on the experience of reading. For example, in the CD-ROM version of Minsky's *Society of Mind* (1996), the page, which is limited to about two hundred fifty words, is fixed, so that readers must sometimes change pages in the middle of a sentence. In contrast, in the large-format paper version of this book, each page corresponded to a complete, autonomous section; the contents of a section could just as well have been chosen as the "page" unit for this particular CD-ROM. This is especially true because on the screen, the visual disappearance of each page when the reader goes on to the next one creates a feeling of loss that readers must learn to deal with. As Roger Laufer and Domenico Scavetta note, "moving from one screen to another breaks the thread of reading more than turning a page."[7]

To spare readers this feeling of a "disappearance" or loss when changing pages, the engineers responsible for the first computers adopted vertical scrolling as the "normal" display mode in word processing, and it was subsequently used on the Web. In recent years, the major word-processing programs have also allowed users to display text in page format and even in double pages, always showing the page numbers; this offers a span and control of reading equal to those of a book. The same, unfortunately, is not true of the Web, where the only position marker in a text is the slider on the scroll bar, whose position indicates the proportion of a text that has been read. There is no small irony in the fact that the publication of text on the Web has led to the replacement of the digital unit of the page number by the analog system of the scroll bar. One can only hope that browsers will eventually offer a more refined system and more flexibility for the display of Web pages.

Publishers of texts on the Web also face the problem of the width of the text column. Until recently, this question did not arise, because the screens available to the public were barely eight hundred pixels wide, which corresponds to a line of approximately eighty characters, the usual width of a block of text in a book. But the length of the lines becomes excessive when the pages are displayed on a screen sixteen hundred pixels wide or more. Paradoxically, this wide screen that is supposed to increase visual comfort may have just the opposite effect, unless the text is formatted in columns; the lines being too long, readers react by speeding up their eye movements and skimming the text, only really focusing on the beginnings of the lines and on a few words here and there.

It should be noted that it was the W3C—the World Wide Web Consortium, which sets the standards for the Web—that was the source of these provisions and that recommended that text in HTML be displayed running from one side of the browser window to the other, filling the screen. By reducing text to a stream of bits, the engineers of the W3C have flouted the venerable tradition of the page as a semantic space of maximum readability. This "de-mediation" of the text could well mark the end of the page, and in so doing, it would accentuate the break with the printed book and encourage an extremely reductive view of textuality. This was clear as soon as the World Wide Web appeared, according to Roy Harris, an expert in the history of written language: "With the computer, we risk letting ourselves

Wall-to-wall text. This page from the W3C site demonstrates the challenges the disappearance of the page and the absence of stable landmarks pose for reading. The format chosen by the W3C engineers certainly allows perfect interoperability between various media, but to the detriment of reading comfort. Faced with such long lines of text, readers tend to skim the text at the beginning of the lines or to read randomly rather than continuously. (http://www.w3.org/TR/2007/REC-webcgm20-20070130)

be convinced that all writing can be reduced to a pattern of black dots on a screen."[8] Yet the white margins surrounding the text are not useless space to be dispensed with; this space delimits the text and allows the eye to rest from the tension caused by reading. A page without margins is an aberration that forces readers to constantly resize their browser window according to the sites they visit.

Much to the satisfaction of readers, however, the major suppliers of text circumvent these recommendations, displaying their text in columns. This is the case for the vast majority of major newspapers and blogs. Similarly, Google, Yahoo, Lycos, and MSN display their news in columns of about 800 pixels. In newspapers and magazines published on the Web, the page most often corresponds to a complete article. This is a very satisfactory solution for relatively short texts, but when a text reaches a certain length, it is often divided into secondary units.

In contrast, scholarly journals usually present articles in a single block. Some of them, without breaking up the physical unit of the text, introduce separation marks corresponding roughly to the length of a printed page, which gives readers useful markers to guide their reading and enables them to refer to specific passages. Others have further refined the ability to locate material by numbering the paragraphs, as at http://www.digitalhumanities .org/dhq/vol/001/1/index.html.

In another refinement, some newspapers display text using the full height of the screen divided into two or three columns under thirty characters in width; in addition to excellent readability, this presentation has the advantage of reducing to a minimum the need for scrolling; see, for example, iht.com and www.lefigaro.fr.

Small collectives are also attempting to adapt the literary text to the screen by placing it in sophisticated environments built using Adobe and Macromedia Flash. In providing access to texts by means of a series of manipulations, these publishers are attempting to place the activity of reading within the framework of a ritual reminiscent of the actions readers carry out in the physical world when they start reading a book (see, for example, revuebordel.com).

Newspapers are also coming to the conclusion that the reading experience is more complete when readers are able to leaf through pages in a PDF format, and they are asking their subscribers to pay a premium for this format; see, for example, www.nytimes.com, www.lemonde.fr, and www.elpais.com. Many magazines are also exploring this format, inviting would-be subscribers to "Flip through the pages and browse headlines just as you would the newspaper" (www.newsstand.com, May 2007). Some magazines are even using this format to reach a young readership, which is something of a paradox and a testament to the enduring power of the double page of the codex. The rationale for this editorial choice is that when they must click page after page to discover the contents of a magazine, readers cannot miss a section or—more important for the publisher—a page of advertising (see, for example, www.papiervirtuel.com, http://issuu.com and *Mlle Figaro*, the supplement of the French newspaper *Le Figaro*, at http://figaro.vr.myvirtualpaper.com). In addition, formatting the text in a closed virtual space that is analogous to the book offers the reader the sensation of closure and fulfillment frequently associated with the printed codex. This format also allows readers to refer to specific sections when talking about their experience.

The Web is thus becoming a hybrid world, offering readers the limitless possibilities of an open space while still providing closed entities reminiscent of the codex, in which the voice of an author or the choices of an editor (in the case of a magazine) can best be approached.

35

On the Fragment

A book is implicitly a totality, which readers should in principle read in its entirety in order to assimilate a subject or the mental configuration characteristic of an author on a particular subject. As Horace said, "let the work be anything you like, but at least let it be a single thing."[1] In hypertext, on the contrary, the text no longer exists as a whole or in a single flow but is parceled out in segments or fragments. According to Jerome McGann, this may well be its essence: "a hypertext is not organized to focus attention on one particular text or set of texts. It is ordered to disperse attention as broadly as possible."[2] Yet printed matter has for centuries included texts designed for noncontinuous reading, such as Michel de Montaigne's *Essais* and Blaise Pascal's *Pensées*.

The fragment as a literary form was theorized by Friedrich Nietzsche, for whom "the deepest and most abiding works will certainly always have something of the aphoristic and unexpected nature of Pascal's *Pensées*."[3] Nietzsche's predilection for the fragment was the result of a deliberate choice in favor of surprise, as summed up in this couplet: "Be brief; let me guess / lest you weary the pride of my mind."[4] Pascal Quignard, who has also written fragments, is ambivalent about the genre. For him, "fragmentation is violence done or undergone, a cancer that corrupts the unity of a body and breaks it down, as it breaks down all attempts at attention and thought on the part of anyone seeking to look at it."[5] He does see advantages in the fragment, however: namely, that it enables the constant renewal of the narrator's stance and that it addresses the reader in a sudden, striking way.

For Roland Barthes, the fragment is conducive to the play of differences and undecidability, creating "explosions" of reading; it clearly belongs to the elite order of the "writerly text," as opposed to the "readerly text," which is dominated by the demand of traditional writing for coherence and plenitude.[6] This is why he consistently chose the form of the fragment for writing his most intimate works. Therefore, it is worth considering the fact that several years after his death, the complete works of this theorist of the poetics of the fragment were published in four volumes in strict chronological order (edited by Éric Marty), so that it is now possible to read or reread every text, every interview, every note by Barthes in relation to the writings that preceded and followed it. Brought together in one book, unified by a single typography and a single layout, and beautifully presented, these "fragments" written over the years do not produce the effect of "torn apart and dispersed" members, which is in principle what fragments are. Quite the contrary. Each one of the texts, surrounded by those written before and after, is now part of the higher organic entity of the "complete works"; far from being a piece of a lost whole, each fragment becomes a trace of an intellectual journey, an episode in the story of a life, a piece in a very coherent mosaic that forms a portrait of a mind in action. The effect created by reading this work is thus ultimately brought back to the person of the author, whose production forms the raw material of an intellectual biography.

Once they are brought together in the material structure of a book, then, even texts initially conceived as fragments can no longer be read as disconnected pieces, since the nature of the collection in which they are included and their connection with the author automatically play a unifying role. Fragments in the world of the book and printed matter are thus always elements of a unified work, and they are read as such. Since the fragment uses asyndeton and discontinuity to produce its meaning effects, however, some of the markers of cohesion that would enable readers to easily relate each fragment to the preceding one and allow a perfectly consistent and continuous reading may be missing.

The situation is often completely different with regard to reading hypertext on the screen, where, without the concept of the book or at least of an entity unified by a single layout and a single intention, each fragment is isolated, a pure atoll of meaning the reader happens upon by activating a chance sequence of links. This is especially true of navigation on the Web, where every click on a link can take readers farther and farther from their initial context, and where attention and comprehension are active only for a very short time. While the printed text represents the triumph of the dominant idea and coherence, hypertext gives readers—and authors—the freedom of conversationalists. It opens the door to abrupt changes of subject, to drifting, to unfettered association.

Since the hypertext fragment is an element detached from context, a flower cut off from the environment in which it was rooted, readers have to recreate the contextual elements that give it life and enable it to be understood. They have to rediscover the flower in the petal, and the garden behind the flower—a delicate operation, in which there is serious danger of achieving a fragmentary, partial understanding, of taking the petal not for an element of a particular flower, but for an undifferentiated scrap of vegetable matter. Because of the additional investment it demands of the reader, the hypertext fragment can thus encourage superficial readings, quickly depleted as a result of the effort of producing and constantly renewing the context of reception. Reading then becomes an orgy of zapping, with all the regressive and infantile traits this behavior entails—as in Sven Birkerts's disenchanted statement: "This user, at least, has not been able to get past the feeling of being infantilized."[7]

36

The Body of the Text

If reading a literary hypertext poses real challenges to the reader, the situation is hardly more comfortable for the intrepid author who sets out to write an article or a book with a fragmented structure in hypertext. How should the flow of the text be broken up? When is the right time to start a new development on a new page, to bring forth another rhizome in an expanding structure, or to create a link to another fragment? Writing a hypertext leads to incessant questioning of the very concepts of text and fragment. A paragraph has barely been started when the writer wonders whether it should be segmented, or whether some idea should be linked to another page. Is the text already too long? Has a concept been introduced that is foreign to the semantic unity of the page and that warrants its own development?

Developing a thought in a fragmented hypertext mode can also result in constant flitting about, which can easily mask problems of internal consistency. There is a risk of a shift in the point of view, or even of contradicting positions stated elsewhere, without realizing it. It is easy to dismiss these concerns, blaming them on an outmoded concept of coherence. But insofar as an author writes for someone, one has to ask why a reader would want to follow the author's thinking on a subject if it lacks unity and contradicts itself.

Another difficulty in the original doctrine of hypertext is that of the title to give to the hypertext fragment—which is indispensable if readers are to be able to select the various fragments from a table. The choice of a title that summarizes the content of the fragment is a complicated matter. How general should it be? A title consisting of only one or two words situates the text at a level of abstraction that almost inevitably disappoints readers and creates an impression of superficiality when they read the corresponding fragment. And once a title has been chosen for one page, it is no longer available for another, unless a sequential number is added, which is rather foreign to the way hypertext functions. Moreover, the more titles there are in a work, the more difficult and cognitively onerous readers' choices become.

There is also the issue of redundancy. In order to enable readers of a hypertext fragment to fully grasp all its ramifications, authors will often be obliged to recontextualize it in detail, since they cannot assume that readers have necessarily read all the related fragments. This will result in the repetition of information or ideas that are considered important but that readers may not yet have encountered in the course of their navigations.

In short, then, writing in hypertext, at least in the opaque and artificially fragmented mode that was idealized in the nineties, seems profoundly foreign to textual reality and to the requirements of reading. Paradoxically, it brings back traditional considerations stressing the affinities between the process of writing and those of cell development and embryogenesis. Far from being doomed, as was believed not long ago, the organic metaphor of the text may thus be revitalized and its modes of expression may acquire a new legitimacy. As Plato wrote: "SOCRATES: At any rate, you will allow that every discourse ought to be a living creature, having a body of its own and a head and feet; there should be a middle, beginning, and end, adapted to one another and to the whole?"[1]

In reality, to the best of my knowledge, the idea of systematically fragmenting texts in order to provide access to their basic ideas separately from one another has been abandoned. The encyclopedia model simply cannot be generalized to all types of texts. A philosophical text or an opinion piece is not an accumulation of "nodes," nor can our thoughts be likened to standardized Lego blocks that can be combined in a variety of different ways. This is especially true for narrative. As Gustave Flaubert wrote in a letter to Louise Colet: "The order of ideas, that is what is difficult."[2] And Paul Ricoeur has shown that a narrative is not just a series of events or actions, but an overall configuration in which various elements are linked together in significant ways.[3] If a textual structure is not reducible to the sum of its parts, it follows that the minimum unit of a text that is placed in an open, multilinear hypertext network must contain everything considered essential to the reader's understanding of it. As a textual unit, the paragraph is not at a high enough level to constitute an autonomous entity, except as a summary lead in a news item or an introduction to a short story. In most cases, it is best to keep the reading unit intact, whether it be a chapter of a book or a magazine article.

And that is in fact the most common solution found on the Web today, as we have seen with regard to the concept of the page. Blogs typically align all the entries of a single month in a single page.

The laborious dividing up of hypertext is thus no longer seen as the way to attain Vannevar Bush's ideal (see chapter 15, "Varieties of Hypertext"). It is now search engines that have the task of steering readers to the specific nodes of information that interest them. We will come back to this major transformation of common reading habits.

37

The Decline of the Novel

Perhaps the novel too is in the process
of dying as a form of narration.

—Paul Ricoeur, *Time and Narrative*

In an article on the art of narrative written long before the existence of media studies, Walter Benjamin observed that "the dissemination of the novel
became possible only with the invention of printing."[1] The novel reached its
peak in the nineteenth century, when the mechanization of printing technology, coupled with widespread literacy, led to the primacy of the printed word.
Offering access to other people's ways of life and to diverse worlds of subjectivity, novels became immensely popular and helped to expand the appeal
of continuous reading at a time when the growing popularity of newspapers
could have represented serious competition for the book industry.

The codex format is remarkably congruent with the narrative form. Like
the narrative, it has a certain scope (a book must have at least forty-nine
pages to be recognized as such according to UNESCO's criteria) and a readily
identifiable beginning, middle, and end. There is also a similarity in terms
of the virtual space created by the novel, which is a closed world, like the
book, and whose plot unfolds at the same time pages are turned. Walter Ong
observes that "With print, tight plotting is extended to the lengthy narrative,
in the novel from Jane Austen's time on, and reaches its peak in the detective
story."[2] It is thus not surprising that in common usage the novel is seen as the

epitome of the book and that the reading experience is by default associated with this genre.

As a medium, the book is imbued with the experiences of pleasure and intellectual discovery we have had thanks to it. This is illustrated by a character in *Mauve Desert*, a novel by Nicole Brossard: "'Love books,' she constantly repeated to her students, 'for you never know by what chance encounter, at the turn of a phrase your life can find itself transformed.'"[3] Expressing the same idea, the anthropologist René Girard at the age of eighty still testified to the appeal of the book and its transformative power: "I always have a feeling that the book I am reading is going to transform my entire life."[4]

In recent years, however, readers have been increasingly reluctant to immerse themselves in closed fictional worlds. Already in *Of Grammatology* (originally published in 1967), Jacques Derrida[5] pointed out the cracks that were accumulating in the body of the novel because its intrinsic linearity was being discredited. In the same vein, another philosopher, Jean-François Lyotard, described his ideal book as follows: "A good book . . . would be . . . a book that the reader could pick up at any point, and in any order."[6] Even in the cinema, whose success depends on the narrative line, there is increasing rejection of the linear narrative. Federico Fellini, for example, enjoyed comics precisely for their capacity to escape the constraints of film: "The comics that interest me are the ones that are the least like cinema, because they cannot be transposed to it."[7] With the advent of the digital society, these centrifugal tendencies have been accelerating. Peter Greenaway envied writers who had escaped the constraints of linearity: "The linear pursuit—one story at a time chronologically—is the standard format of cinema. Could it not travel on the road where Joyce, Eliot, Borges, and Perec have already arrived?"[8]

If "to write is to secrete words within that great category of the continuous which is narrative,"[9] the novel may indeed be a genre in peril, insofar as the computer screen, which is becoming the new space of reading, tends to redefine the parameters of that activity. Instead of being carried away on the deep-sea voyage of reading a book, a voyage that ends only with the last page, Web users are surfing on a dissipative structure with no boundaries and no center; constantly threatened with information overload, they surf through pages, skimming frenetically, searching for semantic events that will be able to hold their attention for a few moments, as in a disjointed conversation.

The novel also has to face competition from other media and the redefinition of the cultural landscape. In 1936 Walter Benjamin foresaw that the growing importance of information was dangerous for the novel and would threaten its survival. What would he say today, when twenty-four-hour information channels have transformed the news into a daily mix involving a number of favorite characters that have become as familiar as the heroes of the novels of our childhood: crowned heads, terrorists, politicians, stars of stage and screen, businessmen, crooks, victims, enforcers of the law, and the rest. This narrative backdrop that is constantly evolving, sometimes with hour-by-hour developments and spectacular police or military operations, has a growing audience of loyal viewers whom it holds spellbound, as serial novels once held their readers.

As if that were not enough, television networks convince ordinary people to live on camera for weeks in situations that involve them in emotional or competitive relationships with various partners. Contemporary viewers thus have round-the-clock access to a variety of narrative threads that enable them to imbue their lives with a sensation of duration and enhance their own uneventful routine with events that mark the lives of others—with the additional advantage that these are true stories.

38

The Rise of the Blog

Public esteem is the nurse of the arts, and all
men are fired to application by fame.

—Cicero, *Tusculan Disputations*

The first blogs (abbreviation for *Weblogs*) appeared in 1997 with the introduction of software that made it easy to maintain and update personal journals on the Web. Thanks to this technology and free hosting sites, anyone
can now post their views on the Web. According to Dave Winer, one of the
first bloggers, the essence of the blog is to convey "the unedited voice of a
single person."[1] Every entry of a blog is normally followed by a link so that
readers can respond to the blogger's comments. An interesting entry may
thus give rise to hundreds of comments, to which the blogger may respond
in subsequent entries. As a result, the distance between author and reader
is substantially reduced. More than a personal journal, the blog has given
rise to a kind of writing in several voices, or more precisely, a kind of public
writing with integrated feedback and an applause meter. Still immature and
plagued by excesses and blunders, the medium is nevertheless finding its way
through the accelerated mutual education of authors and readers.

The phenomenon of blogs has grown steadily, with BlogPulse indexing
about one hundred thousand new blogs per day in May 2007. Thanks to search
tools such as BlogPulse and Technorati, it is possible to follow the evolution of
this universe and even to produce graphs showing the frequency of a particular

term over a given period; this makes it possible to take the pulse of the blogo-sphere and to carry out elementary sociological surveys, such as comparisons of the popularity of political personalities, of the use of terms such as *liberal* versus *conservative* on the American scene, or of voting intentions during the referendum in France on the constitution of the European Union.

There are blogs on every subject: politics, sports, health, entertainment, technology, trivia. Some are like diaries in which people attempt to unders-tand themselves by reflecting on their relationship with themselves and others—which raises the question of the separation of public and private spheres. Most are dedicated to very specialized fields and maintained by ex-perts. These blogs meet the need of people to discuss subjects that interest them or involve their area of expertise. Finally, many blogs simply repeat the content of the major media, generally with a very definite ideological slant, attracting visitors who share the same views and who read these blogs pre-cisely to find a reflection of their own ideology. By reinforcing the sense of belonging to a subculture, blogs may be partly responsible for the increasing polarization of attitudes that we are seeing almost everywhere and that could have devastating effects on the fabric of modern societies.

The phenomenal growth of blogs results from the fact that they make it possible for anyone who so desires to be in the limelight and interact with the public, however limited that public may be. In this respect, blogs embody an essential aspect of the new culture. We may see this as an effect of the culture of narcissism that, according to Christopher Lasch,[2] marks our time, but there is more than static self-contemplation in the impulse that drives people to express themselves on the Web. This movement is also part of a new social and cultural context that encourages people to express themselves and assert their differences in every possible way. Gilles Lipovetsky has followed this trend closely: "The process of personalization driven by the acceleration of technology, by management, by mass consumption, by the media, by devel-opments in the ideology of individualism, and by psychologism has carried the dominance of the individual to new heights and broken down the last barriers."[3] This has only intensified with the advent of the computer, which has given rise to Internet-based communities of choice, in which people come together around shared interests.[4] Blogs thus meet our fundamental need for attention—which Cicero had already identified as the supreme reward and prime engine of creation. Whereas for the past five centuries print imposed a steep barrier on would-be writers, the arrival of the Web has completely changed the situation, making it possible for anyone to achieve a certain level of fame, however mediocre it might be.

As people spend more and more time daily reading the blogosphere, blogs will in all likelihood affect our relationship to narrative. With its openness and relative lack of structure, the blog is even more polymorphous than the novel. With its lack of closure, it is consistent with the general trend toward the elimination of the horizon of death from the human experience—a horizon that, according to Walter Benjamin, was the focus of the traditional novel: "What draws the reader to a novel is the hope of warming his shivering life with a death he reads about."[5] Unconcerned with the strong narrative coherence characteristic of great novels, bloggers draw the thread of their writing from everyday life and current events. Fragments written from day to day are unified by the prism of an individual subjectivity: for example, that of a young office clerk in Paris (*Le journal de Max*: http://www.lejournaldemax .com) or an unemployed fifty-year-old man in Buenos Aires masquerading as a woman (*Mas respeto, que soy tu madre*: http://mujergorda.bitacoras .com/2/). With the colorful microsocieties they describe, some blogs have won sizable readerships and even attracted interest from publishers.

It should be noted that readers take for granted that the narrative they are reading is based on the actual experience of the author, which tends to erase all distance between author and narrator. The blog is thus in tune with the public demand for true stories. It provides readers with a unique vantage point on an individual psyche—which has been the basic function of narrative and its source of attraction since the beginning. As Eric Auerbach wrote at the end of his epochal study on the representation of reality in literature: "It is still a long way to a common life of mankind on earth, but the goal begins to be visible. And it is most concretely visible now in the unprejudiced, precise, interior and exterior representation of the random moment in the lives of different people."[6]

39

A Culture of Participation
and Sharing

The economic and institutional barriers that once defined the information landscape are now obsolete. As a result of the Internet, we are moving from a mass-media culture to a participatory culture. The once clear-cut distinction between author and reader is dissolving into a continuum. Millions of citizens who could never have dreamed of having any influence in the old political and cultural order have the means to participate actively in the extraordinary creative ferment made possible by digital communications. This is reflected in the proliferation of resources—texts, archives, photos, and videos—patiently assembled and posted on the Web by amateurs. Many people spend their spare time developing open-source software, which may be used free of charge by anyone. This software facilitates and encourages the creation of products in many fields, providing a nice example of the "virtuous circle" that Lawrence Lessig explores in *The Future of Ideas*.

Nothing better exemplifies this new culture of the digital gift than the success of *Wikipedia*, the "open," "free" encyclopedia. Created by Jimmy Wales and Larry Sanger in January 2001, *Wikipedia* has developed through the spontaneous contributions of hundreds of thousands of volunteers. In five years, this project, which once would have been considered utopian for both its ambitions and its total lack of an economic foundation, contained in September 2008 more than eleven million articles in some 264 languages. Technically, *Wikipedia* is based on a wiki, a computer program that enables users to carry out operations on the Web directly through their browsers. This software allows any Web user to easily create a new entry or modify an existing entry in the encyclopedia database.

There is good reason to be suspicious a priori of a publication that has no editorial committee and lets anyone at all write articles on any subject and even modify existing articles. There have indeed been cases of abuse, which have been widely publicized. Many people are uneasy with such a revolutionary model and like to believe that an endeavor based on such an idealistic conception of human nature instead of the capitalist rationale of profit is doomed to fail. To prevent abuse, *Wikipedia*'s introductory pages provide precise rules and criteria for entries. For example, for an article on an author, that author must have at least two books published by publishing houses or must be cited in a dictionary or encyclopedia. There are detailed instructions on point of view, stating that while strict neutrality is required in the presentation of facts and theories, this does not mean seeking a middle position, giving equal validity to all points of view, or supporting the view of the majority. They also stress that all points of view should be clearly attributed to the parties, movements, or individuals holding them. The instructions aim to ensure that the articles are of the highest possible quality by asking the authors to present facts without bias and to show intellectual rigor and respect for the views of others.

The texts are not signed, and it is generally impossible to know who has contributed to an article; although a history of each contribution is provided, the information is often sketchy—an IP address, if the contributor did not bother to register, or a pseudonym, but rarely the real name. This practice has alienated people in certain fields where the author's signature traditionally plays a major role, such as the arts and literature. In response to the criticism, it should first of all be pointed out that there is nothing wrong with anonymity in itself; this is shown by the fact that some of the most respected newspapers publish unsigned editorials, which are all the more credible because they represent not an individual opinion, but the consensus of a community. Furthermore, this practice encourages expression by lifting inhibitions inevitably created, even among experts, by the idea of speaking *authoritatively* on a question. Finally, because of the anonymity or protection provided by a pseudonym, anyone can take the risk of starting an entry with a mere draft, which will serve as an appeal to future contributors.

In view of the extraordinary vitality of this undertaking of collective knowledge building, the requirement of a signature seems to be a fossil remnant of the discourse of authority that for millennia dominated science, from which it disappeared in the modern era only to migrate to the world of letters, where it culminated in the romantic cult of the genius.[1] It is a requirement that developed with print and the concept of copyright, and has proven inadequate in the today's technological world, where the once-solid boundaries between authors and readers have dissolved into a continuum of networked digital communication.

Wikipedia, more than any other undertaking, reminds us that knowledge is constantly in flux and can never be fixed. Its open editorial structure obliges readers to exercise a healthy skepticism about the information they find there. The ability to consult the history of each article, which contains the various stages it has gone through, encourages this critical attitude. For some entries, the history contains thousands of files archived automatically by the system, through which it is possible to carry out fascinating studies of the sedimentation of knowledge on a particular question or on the negotiation of points of view among the various writers. In 1999 I wrote, "Hypertext makes it possible to envisage, at least as an ideal, the existence of a vast network in which all the knowledge in a field such as genetics, mathematics, or psychology would be gathered, hierarchically organized and constantly updated."[2] What yesterday was utopian has become a vital and dynamic reality that is constantly gaining credibility, especially in the scientific world.

The cultural impact of Wikipedia cannot be overemphasized. It is important from various points of view. First, with its "copyleft" license, the encyclopedia has won a victory over proponents of the total commodification of public space, for whom access to a paragraph of text or an image must always financially benefit a rights management corporation. The success of this initiative tends to confirm the belief in our societies that knowledge and culture belong in their essence to the public sphere and that the future of global society is inconceivable without universal access to shared knowledge. Second, through the active involvement of hundreds of thousands of contributors throughout the world, Wikipedia helps spread principles of mutual respect, impartiality, and rhetorical neutrality that could appreciably raise the general quality of public debate. Finally, by making immediately available information on almost any question, Wikipedia is developing a new relationship to knowledge. The joy of learning has always been a characteristic of human nature, as Aristotle stated: "Learning things gives great pleasure not only to philosophers but also in the same way to all other men."[3] Curiosity has often been smothered, however, by the lack of reliable and up-to-date answers. Today, Wikipedia offers everybody the kind of environment scholars found in the Great Library of Alexandria or in the monasteries of the Middle Ages, where they had access to knowledge and could communicate with people sharing their interests. *Wikipedia* ushers our civilization into a new cognitive ecosystem that should encourage lifelong curiosity. Moreover, by sharing the same virtual space with many other languages, this encyclopedia is leaving behind the national paradigm of past centuries and contributing to dialogue among cultures. In these respects, it is a milestone in the establishment of a planetwide collective intelligence.

40

Toward the Universal Digital Library

> As copies have been dethroned, the economic model built
> on them is collapsing. In a regime of superabundant free
> copies, copies lose value. They are no longer the basis of
> wealth. Now relationships, links, connection and sharing
> are. Value has shifted away from a copy toward the many
> ways to recall, annotate, personalize, edit, authenticate,
> display, mark, transfer and engage a work.
>
> —Kevin Kelly, "Scan This Book!"

Since the early nineties, conferences and journals have been discussing the question of whether the electronic book will one day replace the "real" book. For many people, a "real" book must still be printed on paper, must be able to be held in the hands and taken to the beach or on the subway, and must provide all the tactile and olfactory sensations connected with the materiality of the physical object. By this definition, it is quite obvious that the electronic document will never be worthy of being called a book.

It is interesting to note that a similar debate took place in Rome in the third century of the Common Era. The occasion was the interpretation of a will involving the "books" of the deceased: Did that mean only papyrus scrolls or did it include codices? According to a lawyer of the time, "The codices should also be considered books. The term *book* does not mean a papyrus scroll but a mode of writing for a specific purpose."[1] This judgment puts the question in perspective and reminds us that a book is above all a vehicle for meaning waiting for readers.

The organizing principle of a digital text on the Web is no longer that of the codex. Right: Hubert and Jan Van Eyck, detail from the Ghent Altarpiece (*Adoration of the Mystic Lamb*), 1432. As is typical in medieval paintings, the Virgin Mary is shown reading a codex. The book symbolizes the word of God, and its exaltation is a recurrent theme in religious painting through the Middle Ages and in the early Renaissance.

Just as the codex led to a qualitative leap forward in the world of reading, digitization gives text attributes that were previously undreamed of: ubiquity, fluidity, interactivity, and complete indexation. Thanks to the Web, texts are accessible from anywhere by means of a portable computer or cell phone. This offers contemporary readers portability that would certainly have been envied by the Persian vizier Abdul Kassem Ismail (938–995), who, according to Alberto Manguel,[2] took with him everywhere he went his library of 117,000 volumes loaded on 400 camels trained to walk in alphabetical order. The contemporary Internet user can be in permanent contact with universal knowledge, which has become as omnipresent as the air we breathe.

Fluidity is another special characteristic of the digital world, one we are already unable to imagine doing without. In comparison to the printed book, which is a fixed entity, the digital document is ideally suited to operations such as correction, copying, arrangement of information in serial order, sending, public posting, and discussion in electronic forums. This extreme fluidity is indispensable in a society in which knowledge is evolving daily and the mass of information is growing exponentially. In many fields, people already expect any text they need to read to be available in digital format. Law firms, for example, spend substantial sums of money on the digitization of documents related to their cases. It is obvious that the static world of printed matter cannot meet the needs of a society in which a large proportion of the workforce is employed in producing or processing information. Until recently limited to documents produced through word processing, this fluidity is becoming available on the Web thanks to the wiki format.

The computer has opened up a new dimension of writing through the capacity to interact with others in blogs and forums. Instead of being organized in closely connected hierarchical units, digital texts often have a tabular structure that makes it possible to read all the elements belonging to a particular paradigm, one after another. The organizing principle of a digital text on the Web is no longer that of the codex but rather that of the database, which involves breaking down text into its constituent parts identified by logical tags. Users can thus scroll through all the information on the axis they are interested in. For example, a database on movies, such as imdb.com, can display all films based on the same book, directed by the same director, starring the same actor, or belonging to the same genre. While books can approximate this type of organization through the use of layout and typography, the database has made it possible to systematize this structure and to make all entries accessible on demand, enabling precise searches with a few mouse clicks.

It is impossible to overestimate the impact of search engine indexing technology, which makes it possible to find precise information in a fraction of a second. Indexes that previously required years of work for scholars are now built on the fly by a computer. Thanks to search engines, the Web functions as a gigantic database in which all items can be accessed in isolation, in conjunction with other items, or with the exclusion of certain terms. Through a feedback loop, the increase of information on the Web boosts the power of search engines, leading even more people to post content on the Web. As a result of the search engine's role as intermediary, the content of the Web has quickly become part of the market economy, not only directly but also indirectly, through its use for promotion; the Internet has made it possible to reach a public for books or recordings that were previously almost impossible to sell—a phenomenon that has been called the "long tail," a reference to the shape of a sales graph.[3] This phenomenon will be greatly expanded, as will research on all kinds of subjects, with the advent of the semantic web, where content will be tagged by ontology languages, translating into a com-

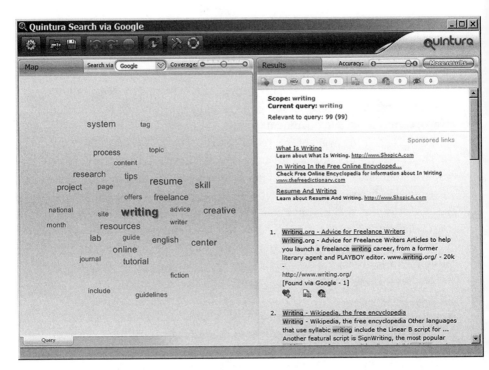

Search engines are the essence of the Web, but most users do not look beyond the first four or five results. For this reason, visual display interfaces are being developed. This example shows the results of a search for the word *writing* using the meta-search engine Quintura (http://www.quintura.com/, February 2007).

mon international vocabulary ideas expressed in various styles and various languages. One of the most ambitious of these ontologies is the IEML developed by Pierre Lévy at the University of Ottawa (ieml.org).

Search engines also have a significant anthropological impact, encouraging the desire for knowledge by making it easy for people to find answers to their questions. This creates a virtuous circle, since the more easily one obtains answer to one's questions, the more tempted one is to ask more questions and do further research. Since the introduction of public education, there has been no invention that has done as much as the Web to raise the intellectual level of society. A culture of questioning is becoming established, and a highly targeted way of reading that was formerly exclusive to scholarly readers is supplanting continuous reading.

There is no doubt that reading will increasingly be carried out on digital media, as any activity tends to seek the ideal conditions for its performance.

While reading was until very recently identified with its natural medium of the book, we now must learn to identify it with the screen: "The book has now ceased to be the root-metaphor of the age; the screen has taken its place."[4] Books, however, will still accompany us for many years, as they are beautiful objects that people will want to keep in their environment, less for reading than as talismans or fetishes invested with sentimental or symbolic value.

In December 2004 Google caused quite a stir in intellectual circles by announcing that it planned to digitize 15 million books in the next few years.

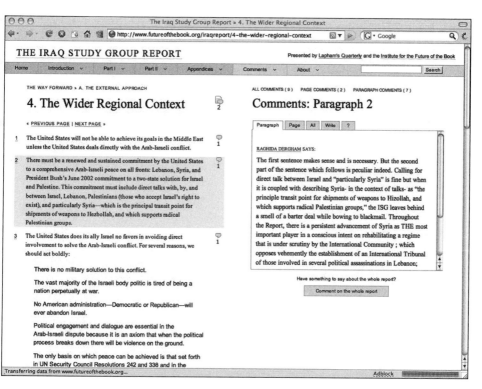

The future of the book. Among the many experiments with text display on the screen, that of the Web site www.futureofthebook.org is very well suited to attentive reading. In the example above, the main text, in this case *The Iraq Study Group Report* (2006), is displayed in the left-hand column. The paragraphs are numbered. In addition to ensuring the stability of references, this layout allows comments on each paragraph to be displayed in a separate window. The highlighted paragraph has been selected by the reader in order to display comments or add the reader's own. Rather than being displayed in its entirety on a single page, the text is segmented into semantic units, which here correspond to the chapters. (Site consulted in February 2007.)

Despite the legal problems the project has encountered, this is certainly the way of the future. In a detailed article in the *New York Times Magazine*, Kevin Kelly convincingly wrote: "Soon a book outside the library will be like a Web page outside the Web, gasping for air. Indeed, the only way for books to retain their waning authority in our culture is to wire their texts into the universal library."[5] In view of the fact that of the 32 million books published since the invention of writing, 10 percent are still protected by copyright, 15 percent are in the public domain, and 75 percent are in legal limbo, he claims that there is a "moral imperative" to scan all books in the latter two categories and to rethink the concept of copyright in terms of the virtual world.

It is indeed important to find a way out of the present paradoxical situation in which we can find on the new medium of the Web practically everything that was published in ancient Rome and Greece and a good part of what was published in many countries in the eighteenth and nineteenth centuries, while texts that are closer to us and more likely to enlighten and enrich our thinking on today's world are kept in their paper prison. The inclusion of these texts in the collective memory of the Web would enhance their topicality, finally making them searchable and accessible by everyone, and the new virtual space would become the twenty-first century's natural extension of the concept of the library created in Alexandria some three hundred years before the Common Era.

Opposition by publishers is all the less justified since the screen is significantly deficient in comparison with the codex in that it lacks physical pages. Vertical scrolling, while suitable for a short text, is not very satisfactory for longer works, because it does not allow readers to quantify the text remaining to be read and thus to manage their reading time, or to go back to the exact place where they left off in a previous reading session. Horizontal scrolling deprives readers of the simultaneous presence of the text read and the text to be read in the screen window. This explains why it is not often used, except in the ergonomics of the e-book, which was designed as a virtual avatar of the book. Although their pagination and polished layout are definitely better suited to continuous reading than to vertical scrolling, e-books have never taken off, since contemporary readers tend to demand that texts be fully integrated into the space of the Web and possess the attributes of ubiquity, interactivity, and fluidity discussed above.

The ideal would obviously be an electronic book in the form of a codex, on which the text could be displayed continuously and through which one could leaf as through a book. It would thus combine the codex's permanent completeness with all the attributes of digital text. Such an object, which Neal

Stephenson envisaged in *The Diamond Age* (1995), has now emerged from the realm of science fiction thanks to the efforts of Joseph Jacobson when still a student at MIT. The E Ink Corporation has already begun manufacturing a high-resolution display material that can be read from any angle without backlighting, using reflected light; it provides as high a contrast as paper and consumes a fraction of the energy required by a traditional screen. Although this text display material has been on the market since 2005 in a new generation of e-book, like the Sony Reader and the Amazon Kindle, it will probably take years before it can be bound into a codex with enough pages to equal a book while having the functions of a computer. In addition to its performance requirements of microprocessors and miniaturization, it would have to have an operating system far more complex than the current ones, since the leafable pages of the codex would have to coexist with the connectivity of hypertext. The result would be a hybrid space for which new metaphors would be needed. In terms of reading, however, the advantages would be spectacular. The space would be infinitely richer and more diverse than that of current screens, with a display capacity commensurate with the number of pages. In addition, the possibility of having a page display the same content indefinitely, if the reader so desired, would give the virtual world a certain stability and allow users to read several works at the same time over days or weeks, as is the case in the world of physical books. This would give new life to the continuous reading characteristic of novels or nonfiction works.

. :: .
:: :: ::

Having reached the end of my investigation, I am aware that I have left many important problems related to the Web untouched or barely broached. My aim was simply to put in perspective the changes taking place in reading, changes that are often ignored because their effects are essentially invisible, but whose consequences for cultural behavior in general will nonetheless be significant. A parallel may be made with the history of the book; the effects of the change from the scroll to the codex were really felt only centuries later, but they played a decisive role in the founding of today's culture. If we can anticipate now the long-term effects of the new media on reading, we will be able to mitigate them by developing more sophisticated technology.

In the digital culture that is being established in front of our eyes, a new form of reading is emerging: gleaning, clicking, zapping, skimming; it is both visual and tabular and does not involve a meditative attitude; rather it focuses on finding answers to questions and rapidly renewing objects on the screen. Above all, by making it possible to combine writing, image, sound, and video, the new computer technologies are undermining the dominant position of language, stripping it of the aura with which it has been invested since ancient times when it was used to magically address the world, to express a relationship to reality, and to hold the tribe under its charm.

Tomorrow's readers will certainly continue to seek out texts to nourish their imagination and their need for analytical reflection and personal growth, but they will also have a greater desire to express themselves, to put forward their opinions, to create links, to put tags on photos, videos, songs, or texts that have moved or interested them, and in short, to play an active role in the social and cultural sphere. The collaborative creative effort that in the last ten years has made a treasure trove of data accessible to everyone through the Web should intensify even more with the contribution of younger generations who were born into the space of this medium.

We must now also strive to ensure that the Internet is accessible in all communities throughout the world. We urgently need to bridge the gap between the developing world and the developed world, so that all people have access to the global network of knowledge and the means to take control of their individual development and that of their communities.

Notes

Chapter 1

1. See Henri-Jean Martin, Elizabeth Eisenstein, Roger Chartier, and Robert Darnton.
2. See J. David Bolter, George P. Landow, Espen J. Aarseth, Roger Laufer, and Geoffrey Nunberg.
3. See Walter J. Ong and Jacques Derrida.
4. See Marshall McLuhan and Régis Debray.
5. Diderot and d'Alembert, *Encyclopédie*, s.v. "Livre." [translation by Aronoff and Scott; such translations are hereafter noted as "our translation"].
6. Borges, *Other Inquisitions*, 103.

Chapter 2

1. "His voice and his tongue were still," Augustine, *Confessions*, 6.3.
2. Saenger, "Manières de lire médiévales."

Chapter 3

1. Blanchot, *Writing of the Disaster*, 33.

Chapter 4

1. Molino, "Le Texte," 22; our translation.
2. Jackson, *Story of Writing*, 23.
3. Curtius, *La Littérature européenne*, 371 our translation.
4. Parkes, *Pause and Effect*, 14.
5. Mallarmé, "The Book," 24.

Chapter 5

1. Quoted in Derrida, *Of Grammatology*, 303.
2. Saussure, *Course*, 23–24.
3. Rayner and Pollatsek, "Phonological Codes."
4. Ong, *Interfaces*, 103.
5. Borges, "Las Kenningar," 43; our translation.

Chapter 6

1. Rabelais, *Gargantua and Pantagruel*, vol. 2, 8.
2. Peignot, "Préface," xi; our translation.
3. McLuhan, *Gutenberg Galaxy*, 231.
4. Dionysius of Halicarnassus, *Roman Antiquities*, 3.
5. Olson, "From Utterance to Text."
6. Miall and Kuiken, "Foregrounding, Defamiliarization, and Affect."
7. Quoted by Guitton, *Nouvel Art*, 66; our translation.
8. Cristin, *L'Image écrite*, 39.
9. Cristin, *L'Image écrite*, 43; our translation.

Chapter 7

1. Derrida, *Of Grammatology*, 86.
2. Greimas and Courtés, *Semiotics and Language*, 176.
3. Christin, *L'Image écrite*, 100.
4. Ong, *Orality and Literacy*, 34.
5. Mallarmé, "The Book," 32.
6. See Drucker, *The Visible Word*, and chapter 9 below, "Meaning and Effect."
7. Lukács, cited in Walter Benjamin, "The Storyteller," 155.
8. Barthes, *S/Z*, 30.
9. Sollers, quoted by Denis, "Compte rendu"; our translation.
10. Simon, *The Flanders Road*.
11. Aristotle, *Poetics* 1450B, 8.
12. Aarseth, *Cybertext*, 47.

Chapter 8

1. Dain, "L'Écriture grecque," 622.
2. Martial, *Epigrams*, 10.93; Quignard, *Petits traités*, vol. 3, 31.
3. Roberts and Skeat, *The Birth of the Codex*, 73.
4. Labarre, *Histoire du livre*, 12; our translation.
5. Sirat, "Du rouleau au codex," 21; our translation.
6. Illich, *In the Vineyard of the Text*.
7. Saenger, *Space between Words*.

8. Febvre and Martin, *L'Apparition du livre.*

9. Martin, *The History and Power of Writing*, 153.

10. Mouillaud and Tétu, *Le Journal quotidien*, 56; our translation.

11. Mouillaud and Tétu, *Le Journal quotidien*, 57; our translation.

12. Mouillaud and Tétu, *Le Journal quotidien*, 57–58; our translation.

Chapter 9

1. Greimas and Courtés, *Semiotics and Language*, 47–48.

2. Bakhtin, "Remarques sur l'épistémologie des sciences humaines," 382; our translation.

3. Sartre, *Situations II. Qu'est-ce que la littérature*, 56; our translation. (This sentence has been omitted in the published English translation.)

4. Bransford and Nitsch, "Coming to Understand Things," 86.

5. See Minsky; Rumelhart and Norman; and Schank and Abelson.

6. Minsky, *The Society of Mind.*

7. Valéry, *Cahiers I*, 930.

8. Austen, *Pride and Prejudice*, chap. 3.

9. Olson, "From Utterance to Text."

10. Valéry, *Cahiers I*, 885; our translation.

11. Valéry, *Cahiers I*, 899; our translation.

12. Proust, *Chroniques*, 194; our translation.

13. Iser, *Act of Reading, passim.*

14. Desnos, quoted by Meschonnic, *Pour la poétique*, 53; our translation.

15. The Necker cube is explained in *Wikipedia*, the source of the image presented here. For other examples, see the rich collection in the "Illusions Gallery": http://dragon.uml.edu/psych/.

16. Minsky, *The Society of Mind*, 234.

17. Gombrich, "The Evidence of Images," 65.

18. Richards, *Practical Criticism*, 183.

19. Drucker, *The Visible Word*, 95.

20. Lyotard, "The Dream-Work Does Not Think," 29.

Chapter 10

1. Quignard, *Petits traités*, vol. 5, 151; our translation.

2. Montaigne, *Essays*, 176.

3. Febvre and Martin, *L'Apparition du livre.*

4. Blagden, *The Stationers' Company*, 30.

5. Borges, *Ficciones*, "Pierre Menard, autor del Quijote."

Chapter 11

1. Ducrot and Todorov, *Encyclopedic Dictionary of the Sciences of Language*, 294.
2. Adam, *Éléments de linguistique textuelle*, 31; our translation.
3. Quoted by Genette, *Figures II*, 150; our translation.

Chapter 12

1. Haddad, "L'Autodafé."
2. Ong, *Orality and Literacy*, 95.
3. Thomas Aquinas, *Summa Theologica*, III, 42, 4.

Chapter 13

1. Benveniste, *Problèmes de linguistique générale. II*, 80; our translation.
2. Benveniste, *Problems in General Linguistics*, 209.
3. Murray, *Hamlet on the Holodeck*.

Chapter 14

1. Gadamer, "Zwischen Phänomenologie und Dialektik," 6; our translation.
2. Sterne, *Tristram Shandy*, vol. 1, chap. 6, p. 17.
3. Diderot, *Jacques the Fatalist*, 4.
4. Brontë, *Villette*, 689.
5. Twain, *Roughing It*, 340.
6. Queneau, "Un conte à votre façon"; our translation.
7. See, for example, Biron and Popovic, *Un Livre dont vous êtes l'intellectuel* [*A book in which you're the intellectual*] (1998), on trends in French literary theory during the last fifty years.

Chapter 15

1. Genette, *Palimpsests*, 7.
2. Riffaterre quoted in Genette, *Palimpsests*, 2.
3. http://iat.ubalt.edu/moulthrop/hypertexts/HGS/

Chapter 16

1. Landow, *Hyper/Text/Theory*, 1.
2. See an example of typographic play at http://www.year01.com/nomadlingo/zindex5.html.

Chapter 17

1. Goody, *The Domestication of the Savage Mind*, 81.
2. Ibid., 84.

Chapter 18

1. Coover, "The End of Books."
2. Joyce, *Of Two Minds*, 31.
3. http://www.altx.com/thebody/
4. For an anthology of works, see http://www.uoc.edu/in3/hermeneia/angl/ antologia.htm or www.ubu.com.
5. http://iat.ubalt.edu/moulthrop/hypertexts/hgs/
6. http://hypertext.rmit.edu.au/hyperweb/
7. Aarseth, *Cybertext.*
8. Burgess, Hamming, and Markley, "The Dialogics New Media," 67.
9. Parks, "Tales Told by the Computer," 50.
10. Douglas, *The End of Books*, 15.

Chapter 19

1. Gombrich, "The Evidence of Images," 50.
2. Marin, "Reading a Picture from 1639," 19.
3. Gadamer, "Zwischen Phänomenologie und Dialektik," 17; our translation.
4. Barthes, *Camera Lucida*, 16.
5. Marin, "Reading a picture from 1639," 24.
6. Sartre, *Situations II: Qu'est-ce que la littérature?* 27.
7. Debray, *Cours de médiologie générale*, 59; our translation.
8. Lyotard, "Taking the Side of the Figural," 34.
9. Saint-Martin, *Semiotics of Visual Language*, 71.
10. Gombrich, "The Evidence of Images," 89.
11. Everaert-Desmedt, *Le Processus interprétatif*, 89; our translation.
12. Umberto Eco, *Semiotics and the Philosophy of Language.*
13. Dyens, *Navigations technologiques.*
14. http://www.culture.gouv.fr/culture/arcnat/fr/
15. http://maptube.org/home.aspx/
16. http://www.incident.net/v6/timeline

Chapter 20

1. Flaubert, *Correspondance*, 13 February 1880.
2. Flaubert, *Correspondance*, letters to Duplan, 10 and 12 June 1862.
3. Baudelaire, *Mon cœur mis à nu*, 1295; our translation.
4. Sartre, *The Psychology of Imagination*, 75.
5. Butor, "Littérature et peinture," 28; our translation.

Chapter 21

1. Debray, *Vie et mort de l'image.*
2. Strabo, *Geography*, 2.5.11.

3. Châtelain and Pinon, "L'Intervention de l'image," 238.
4. Ibid.; our translation.
5. See Tufte, *Visual Display of Quantitative Information,* 41. Also available in Wikipedia.
6. See, for example, the series published by Icon Books in Cambridge, which includes *Baudrillard for Beginners, Derrida for Beginners, Hegel for Beginners,* and dozens of similar titles.
7. Kerckhove, *The Skin of Culture,* 108.
8. Lanham, *The Economics of Attention,* 110.
9. For examples and analyses, see the works of Edward Tufte.
10. Bolter, "Ekphrasis, Virtual Reality, and the Future of Writing," 256.
11. Mitchell, *Picture Theory,* 16.

Chapter 22

1. Catach, *La Ponctuation*; our translation.
2. Parkes, *Pause and Effect*; Saenger, *Space between Words.*
3. Drillon, *Traité de la ponctuation française.*
4. Parkes, *Pause and Effect,* 53.

Chapter 23

1. Other methods very similar to that of the MLA have been developed, notably the *Chicago Manual of Style* and the American Psychological Association (APA) style.
2. Chartier, "Dispositif de rigueur," ix; our translation.
3. Quignard, *Petits traités,* vol. 3; our translation.

Chapter 24

1. Larbaud, *Ce vice impuni, la lecture.*
2. Hesse, "Lektüre im Bett," 265; our translation.
3. Cervantes, *Don Quixote,* 58 (Part 1, chap. 1).
4. Ronsard, 33.

Chapter 25

1. Rousseau, *The Confessions,* 242.
2. Rousseau, *Julie, or the New Heloise,* 46.
3. Certeau, "La Lecture absolue."
4. See Darnton, *The Great Cat Massacre,* 249.
5. Flaubert, *Dictionary of Accepted Ideas,* 35.
6. Ibid., 30.
7. Chartier, *Histoires de la lecture,* 275; our translation.
8. Sartre, title of chapter 3 in *Situations II.*

9. Iser, *The Act of Reading*, 34.
10. Enzensberger, "A Modest Proposal," 11.
11. Pennac, *Reads like a Novel*, 145–46.

Chapter 26

1. Valéry, *Cahiers I*, 29–30; our translation.
2. Virgil, *Georgics*, 2.41.
3. Dante, *Paradiso* 2.1; Longfellow translation, 8.
4. Céline, quoted in Drillon, *Traité de la ponctuation française*, 75; our translation.
5. Heyer, "The Creative Challenge of CD-ROM," 347.

Chapter 27

1. Zumthor, *Langue, texte, énigme*, 18; our translation.

Chapter 31

1. For example, visit the British Library at http://www.bl.uk/onlinegallery/ttp/ttpbooks.html and explore the Lindisfarne's Gospels, Vesalius's book of anatomy and many other beautiful books.

Chapter 33

1. Valéry, *Cahiers I*, 912.
2. Lipovetsky, "Zappeur et sans reproche," 69; our translation.
3. Debray, *Cours de médiologie générale*, 78; our translation.
4. Foucault, *The Order of Things*, 46.
5. Gide, *Journals*, 9.
6. Certeau, *L'Invention du quotidien*.
7. Barthes, "Entretien avec Jacques Chancel," 345; our translation.
8. Montaigne, *Essays*, 54.

Chapter 34

1. Zali, *L'aventure des écritures*, 40.
2. Stoicheff and Taylor, *The Future of the Page*.
3. Moulthrop; Harpold; Barthes; Aarseth; and Kearsley, *Hypertext*.
4. Baudin, *L'Effet Gutenberg*, 56; our translation.
5. Schneiderman and Kearsley, *Hypertext Hands-On!*
6. ise.uvic.ca
7. Laufer and Scavetta, *Texte, hypertexte et hypermédia*,87; our translation.
8. Harris, *La Sémiologie de l'écriture*, 141; our translation.

Chapter 35

1. Horace, 7.
2. McGann, *Radiant Textuality*, 71.
3. Nietzsche, quoted in Susini-Anastopulos, *L'Écriture fragmentaire*, 448; our translation.
4. Nietzsche, *Dithyrambs of Dionysus*, 35.
5. Quignard, *Une Gêne technique*, 23; our translation.
6. See notably *A lover's discourse: fragments*; Roland Barthes.
7. Birkerts, *The Gutenberg Elegies*, 162.

Chapter 36

1. Plato, *Phaedrus,* (264c), 78.
2. Flaubert, *Correspondance,* vol. 2, 536; our translation.
3. Ricoeur, *Time and Narrative*.

Chapter 37

1. Benjamin, "The Storyteller," 147.
2. Ong, *Orality and Literacy*, 133.
3. Brossard, *Mauve Desert*, 114.
4. Girard, *Les origines de la culture*, 44; our translation.
5. Derrida, *Of Grammatology*.
6. Lyotard, "Taking the Side of the Figural," 42.
7. Lacassin, *Pour un neuvième art*; our translation.
8. Greenaway, quoted in Manovich, *The Language of New Media*, 237.
9. Barthes, *Critical Essays*, 173.

Chapter 38

1. Winer, quoted in *The Economist*, "It's the links, stupid," April 20th, 2006 (online).
2. Lasch, *The Culture of Narcissism*.
3. Lipovetsky, *Ère du vide*, 26; our translation.
4. Castells, *The Internet Galaxy*.
5. Benjamin, "The Storyteller," 156.
6. Auerbach, *Mimesis*, 488.

Chapter 39

1. Foucault, *The Archaeology of Knowledge*, 221–22.
2. Vandendorpe, *Du papyrus à l'hypertexte*, 243.
3. Aristotle, *Poetics*, 1448b.

Chapter 40

1. Quoted in Roberts and Skeat, *The Birth of the Codex*, 32; our translation.
2. Manguel, *A History of Reading*, 193.
3. Anderson, "The Long Tail."
4. Illich, *In the Vineyard of the Text*, 3.
5. Kelly, "Scan This Book!"

References

Aarseth, Espen J. *Cybertext. Perspectives on Ergodic Literature*. Baltimore, Md.: Johns Hopkins University Press, 1997.

Adam, Jean-Michel. *Éléments de linguistique textuelle*. Liège, Belgium: Mardaga, 1990.

Anderson, Chris. "The Long Tail." *Wired* (October 2004): 170–77.

Aristotle. *Poetics*. Translated by Samuel Henry Butcher. Mineola, N.Y.: Dover, 1997.

Asimov, Isaac. "The Ancient and the Ultimate." In *The Tragedy of the Moon*. 171–81. Doubleday, 1973.

Auerbach, Eric. *Mimesis: The Representation of Reality in Western Literature*. Translated by W. Trask. New York: Doubleday Anchor, 1953.

Austen, Jane. *Pride and Prejudice*. New York: W. W. Norton, 2000.

Bakhtin, Mikhail. "Remarques sur l'épistémologie des sciences humaines." In *Esthétique de la création verbale*. Paris: Gallimard, 1984.

Barthes, Roland. *Camera Lucida: Reflections on Photography*. Translated by Richard Howard. New York: Farrar, Straus and Giroux, 1981.

———. *Critical Essays*. Translated by Richard Howard. Evanston, Ill.: Northwestern University Press, 1972.

———. "Entretien avec Jacques Chancel." In *Œuvres complètes*, vol. 3, edited by Éric Marty. Paris: Seuil, 1995.

———. *A Lover's Discourse: Fragments*. Translated by Richard Howard. New York: Hill and Wang, 1978.

———. *S/Z*. Translated by Richard Miller. New York: Hill and Wang, 1974.

———. *Roland Barthes*. Translated by Richard Howard. New York: Hill and Wang, 1977.

Baudelaire, Charles. "*Mon cœur mis à nu*." *Œuvres complètes*. Paris: Gallimard, 1961.

Baudin, Fernand. *L'Effet Gutenberg*. Paris: Éditions du Cercle de la librairie, 1994.

Benjamin, Walter. "The Storyteller," translated by Harry Zohn. In *Selected Writings*. Vol. 3, *1935–1938*, edited by Howard Eiland and Michael W. Jennings. Cambridge, Mass.: Harvard University Press, 2002.

Benveniste, Émile. *Problèmes de linguistique générale*, vol. 2. Paris: Gallimard, 1974.

———. *Problems in General Linguistics*. Translated by Mary E. Meek. Coral Gables, Fla.: University of Miami Press, 1971.

Bergson, Henri. *Laughter: An Essay on the Meaning of the Comic*. Translated by Cloudsley Brereton and Fred Rothwell. New York: Macmillan, 1911.

Birkerts, Sven. *The Gutenberg Elegies. The Fate of Reading in an Electronic Age*. Boston: Faber and Faber, 1994.

Biron, Michel, and Pierre Popovic. *Un Livre dont vous êtes l'intellectuel*. Montréal: Fides, 1998.

Blagden, Cyprian. *The Stationers' Company: A History, 1403–1959*. London: Allen, 1960.

Blanchot, Maurice. *The Writing of the Disaster*. Translated by Ann Smock. Lincoln: University of Nebraska Press, 1995.

Bolter, Jay David. "Ekphrasis, Virtual Reality, and the Future of Writing." In *The Future of the Book*, edited by Geoffrey Nunberg. 253–72. Berkeley: University of California Press, 1996.

———. *Writing Space*. Hillsdale, N.J.: Lawrence Erlbaum, 1991.

Borges, Jorge Luis. *Ficciones*. Buenos Aires: Emecé Editores, 1956.

———. "Las Kenningar." In *Historia de la eternidad*. 43–68. Buenos Aires: Emecé Editores, 1953.

———. *Other Inquisitions 1937–1952*. Translated by Ruth L. C. Simms. Austin: University of Texas Press, 1964.

Bransford, J. D., and K. E. Nitsch, "Coming to Understand Things We Could Not Previously Understand." In *Theoretical Models and Processes of Reading*, edited by H. Singer and R. B. Ruddell. 81–122. Hillsdale, N.J.: Lawrence Erlbaum, 1978.

Bringhurst, Robert. *The Elements of Typographic Style*. Point Roberts, Wash.: Hartley & Marks, 2005.

Brontë, Charlotte. *Villette*. Edited by Herbert Rosengarten and Margaret Smith. New York: Oxford University Press, 1984.

Brossard, Nicole. *Mauve Desert*. Translated by Susanne de Lotbinière-Harwood. Toronto: Coach House Press, 1990.

Burgess, Helen, Jeanne Hamming, and Robert Markley. "The Dialogics of New Media: Video, Visualization, and Narrative in Red Planet." In *Eloquent Images: Word and Image in the Age of New Media*, edited by Mary Hocks and Michelle Kendrick. 61–85. Cambridge, Mass.: MIT Press, 2003.

Bush, Vannevar. "As We May Think." *Atlantic Monthly* 176 (July 1945): 101–8.

Butor, Michel. "Littérature et peinture. Travailler avec les peintres." In *Arts et Littérature*, edited by Michel Butor. 15–29. Québec: Université Laval, 1987.

Calvino, Italo. *If on a Winter's Night a Traveler*. Translated by William Weaver. Toronto: Lester & Orpen Dennys, 1981.

Carlut, Charles. *La Correspondance de Flaubert: Étude et Répertoire critique*. Paris: Nizet, 1968.

Carson, David. *2nd Sight: Grafik Design after the End of Print*. New York: Universe, 1997.

Castellet, Josep Maria. *La Hora del lector*. Barcelona: Editorial Seix Barral, 1957.

Castells, Manuel. *The Internet Galaxy: Reflections on the Internet, Business, and Society*. Oxford, U.K.: Oxford University Press, 2001.

Catach, Nina. *La Ponctuation*. Paris: PUF, 1994.

Certeau, Michel de. *L'Invention du quotidien*. Vol. 1, *Arts de Faire*. Paris: Gallimard, 1990.

——. "La Lecture absolue." In *Problèmes actuels de la lecture*, edited by Lucien Dällenbach and Jean Ricardou. 65–80. Paris: Clancier-Guénaud, 1982.

Cervantes, Miguel de. *Don Quixote*. Translated by Walter Starkie. New York: New American Library, 1964.

Chartier, Roger. "Dispositif de rigueur." *Le Monde* (10 April 1998): ix.

——. "Du livre au lire." In *Pratiques de la lecture*, edited by Roger Chartier. 79–113. Paris: Rivages et Payot, 1993.

——. *Histoires de la lecture: Un bilan des recherches*. Paris: Éditions de la maison des sciences de l'homme, 1995.

Chartier, Roger, and Henri-Jean Martin. *Histoire de l'édition française*. 4 vols. Paris: Fayard, 1982–1986.

Châtelain, Jean-Marc, and Laurent Pinon. "L'Intervention de l'image et ses rapports avec le texte à la Renaissance." In *La Naissance du livre moderne*, edited by Henri-Jean Martin. 236–71. Paris: Cercle de la Librairie, 2000.

Christin, Anne-Marie. *L'Image écrite*. Paris: Flammarion, 1995.

Cicero, Marcus Tullius. *Tusculan disputations*. Translated by J. E. King. Cambridge, Mass.: Harvard University Press, 1927.

Coover, Robert. "The End of Books." *New York Times Book Review*, 21 June 1992, 13.

Curtius, Ernst Robert. *La Littérature européenne et le Moyen Âge latin*. Paris: PUF, 1956.

Dain, Alphonse. "L'Écriture grecque." In *Histoire et art de l'écriture*, edited by Marcel Cohen and Jérôme Peignot. 618–31. Paris: Laffont, 2005.

Dante Alighieri. *The Divine Comedy: Paradiso*. Translated by Henry Wadsworth Longfellow. London: Routledge, 1867.

Darnton, Robert. *The Great Cat Massacre and Other Episodes in French Cultural History*. New York: Basic Books, 1984.

Darnton, Robert, and Daniel Roche. *Revolution in Print: The Press in France, 1775–1800*. Berkeley: University of California Press, 1989.

Debord, Guy. *Society of the Spectacle*. Detroit: Black and Red, 1970.

Debray, Régis. *Cours de médiologie générale.* Paris: Gallimard, 1991.

———. *Vie et mort de l'image: Une Histoire du regard en Occident.* Paris: Gallimard, 1992.

Denis, Jean-Pierre. "Compte rendu du Jardin des plantes de Claude Simon." *Le Devoir* (18–19 October 1997): D5.

Derrida, Jacques. *Margins of Philosophy.* Translated by Alan Bass. Chicago: University of Chicago Press, 1982.

———. *Of Grammatology.* Translated by Gayatri Chakravorty Spivak. Baltimore, Md.: Johns Hopkins University Press, 1976.

Diderot, Denis. *Jacques the Fatalist and His Master.* Translated by David Coward. Oxford, U.K.: Oxford University Press, 1999.

Diderot, Denis, and Jean le Rond d'Alembert. *Encylopédie ou Dictionnaire raisonné des sciences, des arts et des métiers.* Paris: Briasson, 1772.

Dionysius of Halicarnassus. *The Roman Antiquities of Dionysius of Halicarnassus.* Vol. 1. Translated by Earnest Cary. Cambridge, Mass.: Harvard University Press, 1960.

Douglas, J. Yellowlees. *The End of Books—Or Books without End?* Ann Arbor: University of Michigan Press, 2000.

Drillon, Jacques. *Traité de la ponctuation française.* Paris: Gallimard, 1991.

Drucker, Johanna. *The Visible Word: Experimental Typography and Modern Art, 1909–1923.* Chicago: University of Chicago Press, 1994.

Ducrot, Oswald, and Todorov, Tzvetan. *Encyclopedic Dictionary of the Sciences of Language.* Translated by Catherine Porter. Baltimore, Md.: Johns Hopkins University Press, 1979.

Dyens, Ollivier. *Navigations technologiques.* Montréal: VLB, 2004.

Eco, Umberto. *Semiotics and the Philosophy of Language.* Bloomington: Indiana University Press, 1984.

Eisenstein, Elizabeth L. *The Printing Revolution in Early Modern Europe.* Cambridge, U.K.: Cambridge University Press, 1983.

Enzensberger, Hans Magnus. "A Modest Proposal for the Protection of Young People from the Products of Poetry." In *Mediocrity and Delusion: Collected Diversions.* Translated by Martin Chalmers. 3–18. London: Verso, 1992.

Everaert-Desmedt, Nicole. *Le Processus interprétatif: Introduction à la sémiotique de Ch. S. Peirce.* Liège, Belgium: Mardaga, 1990.

Febvre, Lucien, and Martin, Henri-Jean. *L'Apparition du livre.* Paris: Albin Michel, 1958.

Flaubert, Gustave. *Correspondance.* 3 vols. Edited by Jean Bruneau. Paris: Gallimard, 1980.

———. *Dictionary of Accepted Ideas.* Translated by Jacques Barzun. New York: New Directions, 1968.

Foucault, Michel. *The Archaeology of Knowledge; and The Discourse on Language.* Translated by A. M. Sheridan Smith. New York: Pantheon, 1982.

———. *The Order of Things: An Archaeology of the Human Sciences.* Anonymously translated. London: Tavistock, 1970.

Gadamer, Hans-Georg. "Zwischen Phänomenologie und Dialektik, Versuch einer Selbskritik." In *Gesammelte Werke*, vol. 2. 3–23. Tübingen: Mohr, 1985.

Genette, Gérard. *Figures I.* Paris: Seuil, 1966.

———. *Figures II.* Paris: Seuil, 1969.

———. *Figures III.* Paris: Seuil, 1972.

———. *Palimpsests: Literature in the Second Degree.* Translated by Channa Newman and Claude Doubinsky. Lincoln: University of Nebraska Press, 1997.

Gide, André. *The Journals of André Gide, 1889–1949.* Vol. 1, *1889–1913.* Translated by Justin O'Brien. New York: Alfred A. Knopf, 1948.

Girard, René. *Les origines de la culture.* Paris: Desclée de Brouwer, 2004.

Gombrich, E. H. "The Evidence of Images." In *Interpretation: Theory and Practice,* edited by Charles Singleton. 35–104. Baltimore, Md.: Johns Hopkins University Press, 1969.

Goody, Jack. *The Domestication of the Savage Mind.* Cambridge, U.K.: Cambridge University Press, 1977.

Grafton, Anthony. *The Footnote: A Curious History.* Cambridge, Mass.: Harvard University Press, 1997.

Greimas, Algirdas Julien, and Joseph Courtés. *Semiotics and Language: an Analytical Dictionary.* Translated by Larry Crist, Daniel Patte, James Lee, Edward McMahon II, Gary Phillips, and Michael Rengstorf. Bloomington: Indiana University Press, 1982.

Groden, Michael. "James Joyce's *Ulysses* on the Page and on the Screen." In *The Future of the Page,* edited by Peter Stoicheff and Andrew Taylor. 159–76. Toronto: University of Toronto Press, 2004.

Groupe μ. *Rhétorique de la poésie, lecture linéaire, lecture tabulaire.* Paris: Seuil, 1990.

Guitton, Jean. *Nouvel art de penser.* Paris: Aubier, 1957.

Haddad, Gérard. "L'Autodafé." In *La Bibliothèque—Miroir de l'âme, mémoire du monde.* 195–201. Paris: Autrement, 1991.

Harpold, Terence. "Conclusions." In *Hyper/Text/Theory,* edited by George Landow. 189–222. Baltimore: Johns Hopkins University Press, 1994.

Harris, Roy. *La Sémiologie de l'écriture.* Paris: CNRS, 1994.

Hesse, Hermann. "Lektüre im Bett." In *Sämtlich Werke,* edited by Volker Michels. Vol. 14, *Betrachtungen und Berichte II, 1927–1961.* 136–41. Frankfurt a.M: Suhrkamp Verlag, 2003.

Heyer, Mark. "The creative challenge of CD-ROM." In *CD-ROM. The New Papyrus: The Current and Future State of the Art,* edited by Steve Lambert and Suzanne Ropiequet. 347–57. Redmond, Ore.: Microsoft Press, 1986.

Hjelmslev, Louis. *Language: An Introduction.* Translated by Francis J. Whitfield. Madison: University of Wisconsin Press, 1970.

Horace for Students of Literature: The "Ars Poetica" and Its Tradition. Edited by O. B. Hardison and Leon Golden. Translated by Leon Golden. Gainesville: University Press of Florida, 1995.

Illich, Ivan. *In the Vineyard of the Text: A Commentary to Hugh's Didascalicon.* Chicago: University of Chicago Press, 1993.

Iser, Wolfgang. *The Act of Reading: A Theory of Aesthetic Response.* Baltimore, Md.: Johns Hopkins University Press, 1978.

Jackson, Donald. *The Story of Writing.* New York: Taplinger, 1981.

Jackson, Shelley. *My Body: A Wunderkammer.* 1997. http://www.altx.com/thebody/ (accessed October 5, 2008).

Jakobson, Roman. *Essais de linguistique générale.* Paris: Seuil, 1963.

Joyce, Michael. *Afternoon, a Story.* Eastgate.com, 1987. CD-ROM.

———. *Of Two Minds: Hypertext Pedagogy and Poetics.* Ann Arbor: University of Michigan Press, 1995.

Kelly, Kevin. "Scan This Book!" *New York Times Magazine,* 14 May 2006. http://www.nytimes.com/2006/05/14/magazine/14publishing.html?pagewanted=1 (accessed October 5, 2008).

Kerckhove, Derrick de. *The Skin of Culture.* Toronto: Somerville House, 1995.

Klinkenberg, Jean-Marie. *Sept Leçons de sémiotique et de rhétorique.* Toronto: Éditions du Gref, 1996.

Labarre, Albert. *Histoire du livre.* Paris: PUF, 1985.

Lacassin, Francis. *Pour un neuvième art: La Bande dessinée.* Paris: U.G.E., 1971.

Lambert, Steve, and Ropiequet, Suzanne. *CD-ROM: The New Papyrus.* Redmond, Ore.: Microsoft Press, 1986.

Landow, George P. *Hyper/Text/Theory.* Baltimore, Md.: Johns Hopkins University Press, 1994.

———. *Hypertext: The Convergence of Contemporary Critical Theory and Technology.* Baltimore, Md.: Johns Hopkins University Press, 1992.

Lanham, Richard. *The Economics of Attention.* Chicago: University of Chicago Press, 2006.

Larbaud, Valéry. *Ce vice impuni, la lecture: Domaine anglais.* Paris: Gallimard, 1936.

Lasch, Christopher. *The Culture of Narcissism: American Life in an Age of Diminishing Expectations.* New York: Norton, 1978.

Laufer, Roger, and Domenico Scavetta. *Texte, hypertexte et hypermédia.* Paris: PUF, 1992.

Lessig, Lawrence. *The Future of Ideas.* New York: Random House, 2001.

Lévi-Strauss, Claude. *The Raw and the Cooked.* Translated by John and Doreen Weightman. New York: Harper & Row, 1969.

Lipovetsky, Gilles. *L'Ère du vide.* Paris: Gallimard, 1983.

———. "Zappeur et sans reproche." *Le Point* (21 March 1988): 69.

Lyotard, Jean-François. "The Dream-Work Does Not Think." In *The Lyotard Reader,* edited by A. Benjamin. 19–55. Oxford, U.K.: Basil Blackwell, 1989.

———. "Taking the Side of the Figural." In *The Lyotard Reader and Guide,* edited by Keith Crome and James Williams. 34–48. Edinburgh: Edinburgh University Press, 2006.

Mallarmé, Stéphane. "The Book: A Spiritual Instrument." In *Selected Prose, Poems, Essays, and Letters.* 24–28. Baltimore, Md.: Johns Hopkins University Press, 1956.

Manguel, Alberto. *A History of Reading.* New York: Viking, 1996.

———. *Reading Pictures: A History of Love and Hate.* Toronto: Alfred A. Knopf, 2000.

Manovich, Lev. *The Language of New Media.* Cambridge, Mass.: MIT Press, 2001.

Marin, Louis. "Reading a Picture from 1639 according to a Letter by Poussin." In *Sublime Poussin.* Translated by Catherine Porter. 5–28. Stanford, Calif.: Stanford University Press, 1999.

———. *On Representation.* Translated by Catherine Porter. Stanford, Calif.: Stanford University Press, 2001

Martial. *Epigrams.* London: Heinemann, 1919.

Martin, Henri-Jean. *The History and Power of Writing.* Translated by Lydia G. Cochrane. Chicago: University of Chicago Press, 1994.

McGann, Jerome. *Radiant Textuality: Literature after the World Wide Web.* New York: Palgrave, 2001.

———. "Visible and Invisible Books: Hermetic Images in N-Dimensional." In *The Future of the Page,* edited by Peter Stoicheff and Andrew Taylor. 143–58. University of Toronto Press, 2004.

McLuhan, Marshall. *From Cliché to Archetype.* New York: Viking Press, 1970.

———. *The Gutenberg Galaxy.* Toronto: University of Toronto Press, 1962.

Meschonnic, Henri. *Pour la poétique.* Paris: Gallimard, 1970.

Miall, David S., and Don Kuiken. "Foregrounding, Defamiliarization, and Affect: Response to Literary Stories." *Poetics* 22 (1994): 389–407.

Miller, Matthew. "Trip." *Postmodern Culture* 7, no. 1 (September 1996).

Minsky, Marvin. *The Society of Mind.* New York: Simon and Schuster, 1985.

———. *The Society of Mind CD-ROM,* Macintosh version. New York: Learn Technologies Interactive, 1996.

Mitchell, W. J. T. *Picture Theory.* Chicago: University of Chicago Press, 1994.

Molino, Jean. "Le texte." *Corps écrit* 33 (1990): 15–26.

Montaigne, Michel de. *The Essays of Michel de Montaigne.* Edited by William Carew Hazlitt. Translated by Charles Cotton. London: Reeves and Turner, 1877.

Mouillaud, Maurice, and Jean-François Tétu. *Le Journal quotidien.* Lyon: Presses Universitaires de Lyon, 1989.

Murray, Janet. *Hamlet on the Holodeck: The Future of Narrative in Cyberspace.* New York: Free Press, 1997.

Negroponte, Nicholas. *Being Digital.* New York: Alfred A. Knopf, 1995.

Nelson, Theodor H. *Dream Machines: New Freedoms through Computer Screens—A Minority Report.* Chicago: self-published, 1974.

———. *Literary Machines: The Report on, and of, Project Xanadu concerning Word Processing, Electronic Publishing, Hypertext, Thinker Toys, Tomorrow's Intellectual Revolution, and Certain Other Topics Including Knowledge, Education, and Freedom*. South Bend, Ind.: Distributors, 1987.

Nietzsche, Friedrich. *Dithyrambs of Dionysus*. Translated by R. J. Hollingdale. London: Anvil Press Poetry, 1984.

Nodier, Charles. *Moi-même*. Paris: J. Corti, 1985.

Nunberg, Geoffrey, ed. *The Future of the Book*. Berkeley: University of California Press, 1996.

Olson, David R. "From Utterance to Text: The Bias of Language in Speech and Writing." *Harvard Educational Review* 47, no. 3 (1977): 257–81.

Ong, Walter J. *Interfaces of the Word*. Ithaca, N.Y.: Cornell University Press, 1977.

———. *Orality and Literacy: The Technologization of the Word*. London: Methuen, 1982.

Parkes, Malcolm Beckwith. *Pause and Effect: An Introduction to the History of Punctuation in the West*. Berkeley: University of California Press, 1993.

Parks, Tim. "Tales Told by the Computer." *New York Review of Books* 49, no. 16 (24 October 2002): 49–51.

Pascal, Blaise. *Pascal's Pensées*. Translated by H. F. Stewart. New York: Pantheon, 1950.

Paulhan, Jean. *Les Hain-Tenys*. Paris: Gallimard, 1938.

Peignot, Charles. Preface to *De plomb, d'encre et de lumière*. Paris: Centre d'étude et de recherche typographique in collaboration with l'Imprimerie nationale, 1982.

Pennac, Daniel. *Reads like a Novel*. Translated by Daniel Gunn. London: Quartet, 1994.

Perec, Georges. *Life: A User's Manual*. Translated by David Bellos. Boston: D. R. Godine, 1987.

Plato. *Symposium and Phaedrus*. Translated by Benjamin Jowett. New York: Dover, 1994.

Poulain, Martine. "Scènes de lecture dans la peinture, la photographie, l'affiche, de 1881 à 1989." In *Discours sur la lecture*, edited by Anne-Marie Chartier and Jean Hebrard, 427–63. Paris: BPI-Centre Georges-Pompidou, 1989.

Prince, Gerald. "Introduction to the Study of the Narratee." In *Reader-Response Criticism*, edited by Jane Tompkins. 7–25. Baltimore, Md.: Johns Hopkins University Press, 1981.

Proust, Marcel. *Chroniques*. Paris: Gallimard, 1949.

Queneau, Raymond. *Cent mille milliards de poèmes*. Paris: Gallimard, 1961.

———. "Un Conte à votre façon." *Contes et propos*. Paris: Gallimard, 1981.

———. *One Hundred Million Million Poems*. Translated and adapted by John Crombie. Paris: Kickshaws, 1983.

Quignard, Pascal. *Une Gêne technique à l'égard des fragments*. Paris: Fata Morgana, 1986.

―――. *Petits Traités.* Vols. 3 and 5. Paris: Maeght Éditeur, 1990.

Rabelais, François. *Gargantua and Pantagruel.* Translated by Sir Thomas Urquhart of Cromarty and Peter Antony Motteux. New York: Alfred A. Knopf, 1994.

Rayner, Keith, and Alexander Pollatsek. "Phonological Codes and Eye Movements in Reading." *Journal of Experimental Psychology; Learning, Memory, and Cognition* 24, no. 2 (1998): 476–97.

Richards, Ivor Armstrong. *Practical Criticism.* New York: Harcourt, Brace & World, 1960.

Ricoeur, Paul. *Time and Narrative.* Translated by Kathleen McLaughlin and David Pellauer. Chicago: University of Chicago Press, 1984.

Roberts, Colin H., and T. C. Skeat. *The Birth of the Codex.* London: Oxford University Press, 1983.

Ronsard, Pierre de. *Lyrics.* Edited by Mervyn Savill. Translated by William Stirling. London: Wingate, 1946.

Rousseau, Jean-Jacques. *The Confessions of Jean-Jacques Rousseau.* New York: Modern Library, 1945.

―――. *Julie; or, The New Heloise: Letters of Two Lovers Who Live in a Small Town at the Foot of the Alps.* Edited and translated by Philip Stewart and Jean Vaché. Lebanon, N.H.: University Press of New England, 1997.

Rumelhart, David E., and Donald A. Norman. *Representation in Memory.* La Jolla, Calif.: Center for Human Information Processing, 1983.

Saenger, Paul. *Space between Words: The Origins of Silent Reading.* Stanford, Calif.: Stanford University Press, 1997.

Saint-Martin, Fernande. *Semiotics of Visual Language.* Translated by the author. Bloomington: Indiana University Press, 1990.

Sartre, Jean-Paul. *The Psychology of Imagination.* Translated by Bernard Frechtman. London: Rider, 1950.

―――. *Situations II. Qu'est-ce que la littérature?* Paris: Gallimard, 1948.

Saussure, Ferdinand de. *Course in General Linguistics.* Translated by Wade Baskin. New York: McGraw-Hill, 1959.

Schank, Roger C., and Robert P. Abelson. *Scripts, Plans, Goals, and Understanding.* Hillsdale, N.J.: Lawrence Erlbaum, 1977.

Searle, John R. "Le Sens littéral." *Langue française* 42 (1979): 34–47.

Shneiderman, Ben, and Greg Kearsley. *Hypertext Hands-On! An Introduction to a New Way of Organizing and Accessing Information.* Reading, Mass.: Addison-Wesley, 1989.

Simon, Claude. *The Flanders Road.* Translated by Richard Howard. New York: G. Braziller, 1961.

Sirat, Colette. "Du rouleau au codex." In *Le Livre au Moyen Age,* edited by J. Glénisson. Paris: Brepols, 1988.

Stephenson, Neal. *The Diamond Age.* New York: Bantam Books, 1995.

Sterne, Laurence. *The Life and Opinions of Tristram Shandy, Gentleman.* Oxford, U.K.: Oxford University Press, 1983.

Stoicheff, Peter, and Andrew Taylor, eds. *The Future of the Page.* Toronto: University of Toronto Press, 2004.

Strabo. *Geography.* Vol. 1. Translated by H. L. Jones. London: Heinemann, Loeb Classical Library, 1917.

Susini-Anastopoulos, Françoise. *L'Écriture fragmentaire: Définitions et enjeux.* Paris: Presses universitaires de France, 1997.

Thomas Aquinas. *Summa Theologica.* Translated by fathers of the English Dominican Province. New York: Benziger Brothers, 1947. http://www.ccel.org/ccel/aquinas/summa.toc.html (accessed October 6, 2008).

Tompkins, Jane, ed. *Reader-Response Criticism: From Formalism to Post-Structuralism.* Baltimore, Md.: Johns Hopkins University Press, 1981.

Tufte, Edward. *Visual Display of Quantitative Information.* Cheshire, Conn.: Graphics Press, 1983.

Twain, Mark. *Roughing It.* New York: Oxford University Press, 1996.

Valéry, Paul. *Cahiers I.* Paris: Gallimard, 1973.

Virgil. *Georgics.* Edited with a commentary by Roger Aubrey Baskerville Mynors. Oxford, U.K.: Clarendon Press, 1994.

Zali, Anne, ed. *L'Aventure des écritures: La Page.* Paris: Bibliothèque nationale de France, 1999.

Zumthor, Paul. *Langue, texte, énigme.* Paris: Seuil, 1975.

Index

Index

Cohen, Jean, 53
Coleridge, Samuel Taylor, 71
column of text, 107, 136–42
comma, 103
comprehension, 40, 64; shuttle of comprehension, 42–43,104. *See also* meaning,
reading, understanding
Constance School, 113
context: 41–43, 49, 56, 115; and hypertext,
77–79, 111, 130; with question and answer,
25; recreated in the text, 8; virtualization, 61
copyleft, 157
copyright, 104, 157, 164
Cortazar, Julio, 26
Council of Trent, 50
Courtès, J., 23, 40
critical edition, 72
curiosity, 157; culture of questioning, 162
Curtius, Ernst Robert, 117, 166

Dante, 117
database, 54, 57, 85, 128, 155, 161
De Kerckhove, Derrick, 99
Debord, Guy, 97
Debray, Régis, 91, 97, 134, 167, 171, 173
deictics, 59, 60
Deleuze, Gilles, 77
Derrida, Jacques, 12, 22, 150, 167, 168, 172, 174
Desnos, Robert, 46
dialogue, 10, 11, 42, 63, 64–68, 71
Diderot, 3, 64, 65, 113, 167, 170
Dionysius of Halicarnassus, 18
Dolet, Étienne, 103
Douglas, J. Yellowlees, 77, 86, 171
Drillon, Jacques, 103, 172, 173
Ducrot, Oswald, 52, 170
Dungeons and Dragons, 67
Dyens, Ollivier, 93, 171

Eastgate, 77
Eco, Umberto, 92, 171
effect, 3, 20, 86, 99, 101; meaning and, 43–48;
visual effects, 81, 92
Einstein, Albert, 22
Eliza, 62
emoticon, 102, 104
emotions: images, 30, 91, 99; vs. neutrality
of text, 18–19
Engelsing, Rolf, 112
Enzensberger, Hans Magnus, 114, 173

epigraph, 63, 78
ergodic literature, 84
Escher, M. C., 46
Estienne, Robert, 103
extensive reading, 105, 112–15, 116, 127

Fellini, Federico, 150
Fighting Fantasy Gamebooks, 67
film, 56, 68, 71, 92, 126, 150
Flaubert, Gustave, 44, 94, 113, 147, 171, 172,
174
footnotes, 105–7
Foucault, Michel, 77, 173, 174
Fra Angelico, 119
fragment, 25, 38, 53, 78, 96, 117, 143–45, 146,
154
Fuchs, Leonard, 98

Gadamer, Hans-Georg, 64, 68, 89
Galen, 97
games, 62, 67–68, 75, 118; vs. novel, 84
Genette, Gérard, 26, 70, 170
Gesner, Conrad, 98
Gestalt theory, 41
Gide, André, 135, 173
Girard, René, 150, 174
glosses, 33, 34, 38, 85, 107
Gombrich, E. H., 88, 91, 169, 171
Goody, Jack, 14, 80, 170
Google, 139, 141, 163
Gospels, 29, 103, 173
Grafton, Anthony, 105
grammar, 16, 17; textual, 42
graph, 98–100, 128
graphosphere, 97
Greenaway, Peter, 150, 174
Greimas, A. J., 23, 25, 40, 67, 168, 169
Groden, Michael, 138
Groupe μ, 24
Guattari, Félix, 77
Gutenberg, 29

hainteny, 13
Harpold, Terence, 137, 173
Harris, Roy, 140, 173
header, 30, 35, 39
Hegirascope, 75, 83
Hesse, Hermann, 110, 172
Heyer, Mark, 118, 173
hieroglyph, 10, 28
Hitchcock, Alfred, 126

CHRISTIAN VANDENDORPE is a professor of Lettres françaises at the University of Ottawa. With a background in classics and semiotics, he has always been deeply interested in the cognitive processes, as is demonstrated by his PhD thesis on the way children learn to read fables (*Apprendre à lire des fables*, 1989). He began to focus on the changes in reading habits provoked by the arrival of hypertext while designing a CD-ROM to help his students perfect their mastery of French grammar (*Communication écrite*, 1995). This led him to write a prototype of the present book in the form of a hypertext and later to publish the proceedings of various conferences on the impact of the new media for the reading of text: *Aides informatisées à l'écriture* (1995), *Hypertextes: Espaces virtuels de lecture et d'écriture* (2002), and *Les défis de la publication sur le web* (2004). He has also published articles in *Poétique, Le Débat, Communication et langages,* and *Protée,* among others. He is responsible for a database of literary dream narratives (www.reves.ca) and is a member of the editorial board of various academic journals, principally www.revue-analyses.org and www.digitalstudies.org.

The University of Illinois Press
is a founding member of the
Association of American University Presses.

———————————————————————

Composed in 10.5/13 Adobe Minion Pro
with Frutiger display
by Jim Proefrock
at the University of Illinois Press
Designed by Kelly Gray
Manufactured by Sheridan Books, Inc.

University of Illinois Press
1325 South Oak Street
Champaign, IL 61820-6903
www.press.uillinois.edu

Unwin Critical Library
GENERAL EDITOR: CLAUDE RAWSON

GOETHE'S FAUST

Unwin Critical Library

GENERAL EDITOR: CLAUDE RAWSON

Goethe's Faust

JOHN R. WILLIAMS

Lecturer in German,
University of St Andrews

London
ALLEN & UNWIN
Boston   Sydney   Wellington

Allen & Unwin, the academic imprint of
Unwin Hyman Ltd
PO Box 18, Park Lane, Hemel Hempstead, Herts HP2 4TE, UK
40 Museum Street, London WC1A 1LU, UK
37/39 Queen Elizabeth Street, London SE1 2QB

Allen & Unwin Inc.,
8 Winchester Place, Winchester, Mass. 01890, USA

Allen & Unwin (Australia) Ltd,
8 Napier Street, North Sydney, NSW 2060, Australia

Allen & Unwin (New Zealand) Ltd in association with the Port
Nicholson Press Ltd,
60 Cambridge Terrace, Wellington, New Zealand

First published in 1987

British Library Cataloguing in Publication Data

Williams, John R.
  Goethe's Faust. — (Unwin critical library).
1. Goethe, Johann Wolfgang von. Faust
I. Title
832'.6 PT1925
ISBN 0–04–800043–4

Library of Congress Cataloging-in-Publication Data

Williams, John R., 1940–
  Goethe's Faust.
(Unwin critical library)
Includes index.
Bibliography: p.
1. Goethe, Johann Wolfgang von, 1749–1832.
Faust.   I. Title.   II. Series.
PT1925.W54   1987   832'.6   87–9255
ISBN 0–04–800043–4 (alk. paper)

Typeset in 9 on 11½ point Joanna by
Nene Phototypesetters Ltd, Northampton
and printed in Great Britain by
Billing and Sons Ltd, London and Worcester

For Elizabeth, Ivor, Bruno

GENERAL EDITOR'S PREFACE

Each volume in this series is devoted to a single major text. It is intended for serious students and teachers of literature, and for knowledgeable non-academic readers. It aims to provide a scholarly introduction and a stimulus to critical thought and discussion.

Individual volumes will naturally differ from one another in arrangement and emphasis, but each will normally begin with information on a work's literary and intellectual background, and other guidance designed to help the reader to an informed understanding. This is followed by an extended critical discussion of the work itself, and each contributor in the series has been encouraged to present in these sections his own reading of the work, whether or not this is controversial, rather than to attempt a mere consensus. Some volumes, including those on *Paradise Lost* and *Ulysses*, vary somewhat from the more usual pattern by entering into substantive critical discussion at the outset, and allowing the necessary background material to emerge at the points where it is felt to arise from the argument in the most useful and relevant way. Each volume also contains a historical survey of the work's critical reputation, including an account of the principal lines of approach and areas of controversy, and a selective (but detailed) bibliography.

The hope is that the volumes in this series will be among those which a university teacher would normally recommend for any serious study of a particular text, and that they will also be among the essential secondary texts to be consulted in some scholarly investigations. But the experienced and informed non-academic reader has also been in our minds, and one of our aims has been to provide him or her with reliable and stimulating works of reference and guidance, embodying the present state of knowledge and opinion in a conveniently accessible form.

C.J.R.
University of Warwick,
December 1979

CONTENTS

PREFACE

The arrangement of this volume follows the guidelines set out in the General Editor's Preface. I have departed from the usual structure by placing the chapter on the reception of Goethe's *Faust* before the commentary section, in order to outline some of the main areas of critical controversy before turning to my own analysis of the text. I have also appended a brief survey of the prosody of *Faust*; the variety of its metres and verse forms is surely unique in dramatic literature, and this is an area that is not often covered fully or systematically in commentaries. The first part of the volume sets out to provide historical information on the Faust legend and on the composition and reception of Goethe's *Faust*, the second part to provide a guide to the understanding of the work. While the overall unity of *Faust* is not disputed, the approach adopted is to consider the two parts of the drama as related but fundamentally different parts of the whole: the first as a mimetic tragedy, the second as a historical and cultural allegory, both enclosed within a *theatrum mundi* framework. It is hoped that this approach will do justice both to the better-known first part of Goethe's *Faust* and to the relatively unfamiliar sections of the second part.

This volume is written both for the specialist student of German literature and for the interested non-academic reader. A wide knowledge of Goethe's works or of German literature is not assumed; what is assumed is a thorough knowledge, or at least a careful reading, of Goethe's *Faust*. Quotations from *Faust* and from other sources (Goethe's correspondence, conversations and other works) have been translated or paraphrased in English, but references have been provided to the original, and line references have been consistently given to the text of *Faust*. It is therefore convenient if readers have access to a *Faust* text that prints line numbers. To readers using an English text, the Norton Critical Edition, *Faust: a Tragedy*, translated by Walter Arndt and edited by Cyrus Hamlin, is particularly recommended, not only for that reason but also because the translation is faithful to the metres and rhymes of the original, and because the edition contains an extensive critical apparatus in English. Stuart Atkins's recent translation (Suhrkamp edition) reproduces the original metres, but does not attempt rhyme. A rhymed and metrical translation of Part One only, by F. D. Luke, is due to appear shortly in the Oxford University Press World's Classics series; Dr Luke has kindly informed me that his version will print line numbers, and will also contain an introduction and notes.

I have used Ernst Beutler's Artemis *Gedenkausgabe* for references to Goethe's works, as the most complete modern German edition of Goethe, with occasional references to the Weimarer Ausgabe where necessary. Students may, however, find volume 3 of Erich Trunz's Hamburger Ausgabe, or its separate printing as *Goethes Faust* (Wegner Verlag), more convenient for reference to the text of the drama. Volume 8 of the Berliner Ausgabe (Aufbau Verlag) is also recommended; while it is less convenient for line references, it contains not only the *Urfaust* and *Fragment* versions but also the paralipomena, together with historical information and notes to the text. Reclam and dtv editions also print line numbers.

It is impossible to ignore completely the vast encrustation of critical literature that has grown around Goethe's *Faust*; it is equally impossible to take account of more than a selection of it in a study like this one. I have referred to a range of criticism in German and English that has seemed to me to offer valuable, interesting, or – occasionally – eccentric readings of the work. In particular, I have drawn attention to recent criticism that has examined the historical and allegorical dimensions of the second part of *Faust* and has, I believe, laid the foundation for a satisfactory overall understanding of a text that has often been too readily regarded as wilfully obscure or haphazard in both its details and its structure.

I have to thank the University of St Andrews for a period of study leave during which this volume was completed. For their help, advice and encouragement during the writing of it, I am most indebted to Jeffrey Ashcroft, Richard Littlejohns, Barry Nisbet, Claude Rawson and, quite particularly, to Francis Lamport. To my wife, Elizabeth, I owe an immeasurable debt of gratitude.

JOHN R. WILLIAMS
St Andrews, November 1986

ABBREVIATIONS USED IN THE NOTES

In the footnotes, references to books and articles are given by means of shortened titles, after the first mention, while full details of titles and publication are provided in the Bibliography. The following abbreviations are also commonly used in the footnotes:

Biedermann	*Goethes Gespräche*, ed. Flodoard Frhr. von Biedermann, 5 vols (Leipzig, 1909–11).
Briefe, HA	*Goethes Briefe*, Hamburger Ausgabe, ed. Karl Robert Mandelkow, 4 vols (Hamburg, 1962–7).
Briefe an Goethe, HA	*Briefe an Goethe*, Hamburger Ausgabe, ed. Karl Robert Mandelkow, 2 vols (Hamburg, 1965–9).
BA	Goethe, *Poetische Werke*, Berliner Ausgabe, 16 vols (Berlin, 1976–81).
GA	Goethe, *Gedenkausgabe der Werke, Briefe und Gespräche*, ed. Ernst Beutler, 27 vols (Zürich, 1948–71).
HA	*Goethes Werke*, Hamburger Ausgabe, ed. Erich Trunz, 14 vols (Hamburg, 1948–60).
WA	*Goethes Werke*, Weimarer Ausgabe, hg. im Auftrage der Großherzogin Sophie von Sachsen, 133 vols (Weimar, 1887–1919).

GOETHE'S FAUST